What is Sociology?

INTRODUCTIONS TO SOCIOLOGY

What is Sociology?

Johann Graaff

OXFORD
UNIVERSITY PRESS

OXFORD
UNIVERSITY PRESS

Great Clarendon Street, Oxford OX2 6DP

Oxford University Press is a department of the University of Oxford.
It furthers the University's objective of excellence in research, scholarship,
and education by publishing worldwide in

Oxford New York

Auckland Bangkok Buenos Aires Cape Town Chennai
Dar es Salaam Delhi Hong Kong Istanbul Karachi Kolkata
Kuala Lumpur Madrid Melbourne Mexico City Mumbai Nairobi
São Paulo Shanghai Singapore Taipei Tokyo Toronto

and an associated company in Berlin

Oxford is a registered trade mark of Oxford University Press
in the UK and certain other countries

Published in South Africa
by Oxford University Press Southern Africa, Cape Town

What is Sociology?
ISBN 0 19 578074 4

© Oxford University Press Southern Africa 2001

The moral rights of the author have been asserted
Database right Oxford University Press (maker)

First published 2001

Commissioning editor: Arthur Attwell
Editor: Inge du Plessis
Indexer: Mary Lennox
Designer: Christopher Davis
Cover designer: Christopher Davis
Illustrators: Natalie Hinrichsen and Tamsin Hinrichsen

Published by Oxford University Press Southern Africa
PO Box 12119, N1 City, 7463, Cape Town, South Africa

Set in 11 pt on 14 pt Bodoni MT Book by Orchard Publishing
Reproduction by Castle Graphics
Cover reproduction by The Image Bureau
Printed and bound by Clyson Printers, Maitland, Cape Town

Contents

Series Introduction

This small book is the first in a series of small books. The series aims to present basic sociology in a somewhat different way. Firstly, it presents foundational sociological topics in modular form, that is, each topic will be presented in a separate book. That gives them considerable flexibility. Topics can be variously combined to fit a wide spectrum of introductory courses. No longer will you need to buy a hugely expensive 600-page textbook of which you use only one quarter of the chapters. With this series you can buy exactly what you want and use all of it. The first five topics will offer introductions to sociology in general (this one); social institutions (education and the family), crime and deviance, population studies, and industrial sociology.

Secondly, each book will be written in such a way that it tells a coherent story with a developing and cumulative theme. Too many textbooks these days are accumulations of vaguely related concepts with no discernible thread or structure to them. Our view in this series is that logical and sequential argument is one of the prime skills students learn at university level. As such, the texts they work with must model that style, and the exercises they do must practice it. In consequence it is important not only that the style of writing be lucid, logical and organized, but also that the exercises in the book be geared towards higher cognitive skills. You will see that the exercises at the end of each book are carefully constructed to test a range of thinking skills.

Thirdly, the various books will deal with issues of some substance in sociology. They will go beyond the elementary concepts that make up a particular problem area. They will introduce students to debates that are current and alive in modern sociology. Clearly, an introductory textbook cannot expose its readers to the full complexity of technical argument. Texts will therefore need to build up a repertoire of technical language and an armoury of concepts as is the case in any discipline. At the same time, there is utterly no reason why such discussions cannot be clear and accessible, written in language that flows and entertains as it educates. Annotated bibliographies can further this aim by indicating those existing sociological works that promote a similarly easy and rich style.

Fourthly, there are many sociology teachers who want sociology textbooks to be more accessible to southern African students, to use southern African examples, and promote something called 'southern African sociology'. While sociological writing in this subcontinent without doubt benefits from the use of southern African references and southern African examples, and this series of books will pursue that practice, the spread of ethnic or cultural groups and ideological convictions, makes the existence of a southern African sociology, in the singular, very doubtful. Rather, we would expect a range of regional sociologies, in the plural. But even then, the influence of global sociological paradigms is so powerful that it is difficult to find anything that could be called distinctively 'southern African'. So, southern African reference points and examples, yes, but southern African sociology(ies), very difficult.

Finally, sociology is a discipline that can reveal, open up, unveil the social world around us in wondrous ways. It is like cracking a secret code. It can make unthought of, even unheard of, connections and links. But it can also be personal and challenging. It can put question marks behind some of our most dearly held beliefs. The sociological journey then can be exciting, surprising, angering, outrageous and scary. It would not be true sociology if it was not.

1 The Nature of Sociology

What is sociology? In a very simple sense, sociology is the study of society, how it works, and how its parts hang together. But there is a lot more to this statement than is immediately evident. Let us take a brief look at why this might be before discussing it in further detail in the rest of this chapter.

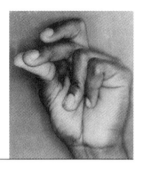

Studying society puts things into a quite new and different perspective. Things that in the normal run of affairs seemed ordinary and natural and mundane suddenly look different and strange. Sociologists call this the *sociological imagination*. It is an angle on things that makes them seem curious, as if we were seeing them for the first time. Ordinary things seem curious when we begin to ask why we do them, what we did 400 years ago, and what people of other cultures do in this regard. Things also seem curious when we link them to unexpected things, for instance, when we say that law-abiding behaviour causes criminal behaviour. Finally, things seem curious when we dig down and discover that they are not what they seem. In these ways sociology makes you blink and shake your head.

A second important but disconcerting sociological task is to reveal the trends, movements and *structures* in society that operate out of human control. (For the moment, a structure is a recurring and regular pattern of social activity.) More than this, it shows how some of these bigger societal waves control our lives in ways that we are unaware of. We all know that somewhere out there, there are frighteningly massive issues like globalization, AIDS, racism, the population explosion or economic depression. But how did these issues originate, how do they change and influence our lives, and how can we influence them, if at all? Put differently, do we control our own lives? And if so, to what extent? These are questions that are central to the business of sociology.

And, having asked these questions, what do the answers look like? What kind of useful information or knowledge does sociology generate? Can it be trusted?

First of all, sociology is a *social science*. It is a science because it takes care about how it puts together its arguments and supports its conclusions. That makes it different from street gossip, from dogmatic assertion, and from religious revelation. But, because it studies human beings and the meanings that they create, it is also different from natural science. Human beings are not rocks or atoms or plants. And they cannot be studied in the same way. So, yes, sociological knowledge is trustworthy and reliable knowledge, but it is constructed in a way that is very different from natural science knowledge.

The kernel of sociological knowledge is *theory*. Sociological theory tells a story about how things hang together, how they work, and why they work. But there are very different kinds of theory. There are hard theories and soft theories. There are functionalist and Marxist theories, and there are macro- and micro-theories. They all tell very different kinds of stories.

So, consider then, the sociological imagination, freedom and determination, science and social science, and theory – these are the some of the major issues in the discipline of sociology. In this chapter I will be elaborating on each of these aspects in a great deal more detail. And in the chapters that follow – those concerning various theories in sociology, namely Marxist theory, functionalist theory and symbolic interactionist theory – we will still pursue these 'big questions'.

As you read further, it is important to keep in mind how these various aspects connect and relate to one another. They link back and forth like a fishing net, each thread connecting to a series of others. As we go I will make some of these links explicit. And I will also challenge you to make further links. Sociology is, as I shall show, a science to the extent that it is a form of logical and sequential argument. So, the new ideas and concepts that you encounter do not just lie around like old shoes in a cupboard. They gradually build up to a bigger and longer story. When you finish reading this book you will be able to look back at the accumulated threads as they are woven into the fishing net. The diagram below shows that interconnection in summary. I shall use it as a reminder as we proceed. At the end of Chapter 5 you will find another diagram summarizing the whole book in much more detail.

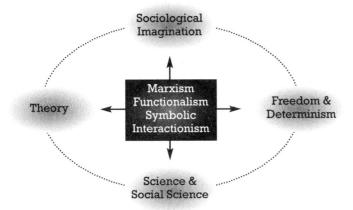

The sociological imagination

In 1959 an eminent American sociologist, C. Wright Mills, wrote a book entitled *The Sociological Imagination*, in which he argued that sociology has a particular approach to the world which brings fresh perspectives and new insights. His lead has been followed by other prominent writers in sociology, like Peter Berger (1966), Anthony Giddens (1989) and Zygmunt Bauman (1990). They have all argued that sociology provides a very particular vision of society. In the following section I will discuss a number of aspects of the sociological imagination, namely, its *relativizing*, *system-relating*, and *debunking* roles. We will see how sociologists can be like magicians, revealing aspects of society that we had not seen before.

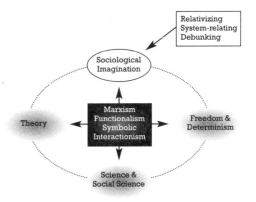

3

Relativizing

The sociological imagination, as I have mentioned earlier, makes ordinary, everyday things seem new and different. In order to show you what this means I want to try a thought experiment with you.

Imagine that you are holding in your hand a can of cooldrink that you like. Cooldrink cans are things we see everywhere. They are stacked in rows in cafés. They stick out of garbage bins or lie in gutters in the street. They are extremely ordinary, banal and boring objects, or so it seems.

Now, take yourself back 200 years in this country. What did people drink in the place of 'cooldrinks' then? There was probably, you might think, no such thing as cooldrink. Did people only drink water (when they weren't drinking something alcoholic, that is)? And did they drink from bottles only, or from cups and mugs (since there was no such thing as a tin can either)? It is quite probable that they would not have bought what they were drinking, but that they had made it themselves.

Seen from that perspective 'having a cooldrink' is quite a curious activity. Those insignificant tin cans make a substantial difference to the way we conduct our lives.

What kind of activity is it when, for example, people sit around a table, talking, 'having a cooldrink'. And how would the social situation change if they were 'having a smoke' with a cigarette in their hand instead of a cooldrink? People 'having a smoke' are different from people 'having a cooldrink'. And they are different again from people 'having a beer' or those 'having a cup of tea' or those 'having a glass of champagne'.

How are they different? People 'having a cup of tea', for instance, might be slightly older people, and their cup of tea would indicate a level of ease and familiarity, probably in the English-speaking (rather than American-speaking) world somewhere. People 'having a glass of champagne', by contrast, would most likely be celebrating something, they might be dressed up in dinner suits and long dresses, and it could be a grand occasion. People 'having a smoke' in the English-speaking (as opposed to the French-speaking) world would probably be younger, their inhaling and blowing out of smoke bringing

out particular expressions on their faces. Cigarettes would probably operate as an important part of their 'image'.

You can see here that cups of tea, cigarettes, glasses of champagne and cooldrink cans are charged with social meaning and symbolism that they have accumulated in our particular society. Sociologists call this process of putting social phenomena into historical and cultural perspective, *relativizing*. And we can ask exactly the same kinds of questions of any social phenomenon. Take, for example, the game of soccer: What did people do for exercise 400 years ago? Did they have a notion of exercise? Where does our notion of 'exercise' come from, or our notion of 'sport'? (Note that you only have to put a word in inverted commas to make it look a bit unusual.)

System-relating

Now consider something else. Where do the components come from that make up this cooldrink: the metal and the paint for the can, and the various ingredients (sugar, caffeine, preservative, colouring). These components probably come from places spread around the globe. What kind of organization was it that brought all of these parts together in a factory, distributed millions of cans to thousands of shops around the country where they are then available to you and me. This boring and banal thing is clearly part of a huge *system* that involves thousands of people and millions of rands, and ties together activities thousands of kilometres apart.

Here is another example. Consider students at a university. Students are not free-floating entities. To understand what the word 'student' means, we have to put them in the context of an academic curriculum that leads to a degree and is run by a large administration. All of this is called a university, and universities fit into the larger economic and political society in particular ways. In this case, the sociological imagination entails placing social phenomena within wider and broader systemic contexts. (In the section 'What is a structure?' on page 9, we shall see how this ties up with the notion of structure.)

An interesting part of the systemic nature of societies is that it ties together some surprising things. There are sociologists, for example, who place great importance on the seamy, underworld, gang-governed side of life. They would say that this reveals a great deal more about a society than its respectable, proper and decent side. Because the two sides fit together, one could not exist without the other. The criminal side of society is an expression, a symptom, of the whole system. For, after all, it is 'ordinary', 'proper' people who buy drugs and pay for sex. Crime is only one side of society, which could not exist without the other 'proper' side. They are two sides of the same coin.

Debunking

Another aspect of our cooldrink can concerns the public image that it carries. It has, in many cases, been the object of a very expensive and skilful advertising campaign. The campaign has, in all probability, attempted to establish emotional and powerful associations in your mind. You will no doubt have been assured of irresistible attractiveness to the opposite sex, or unfailing success in business, or eternal health, or some such miraculous transformation. But there is a private side to this can, which concerns the factories where workers are employed in putting cans together. In some cases they may be badly paid, overworked, physically assaulted, sexually harassed. It is an integral part of the sociological imagination that it reveals the private, grubby, questionable side of life. It shatters the image of upright, morally pure citizens that is often presented in the media. (Satirical magazines like *Mad* magazine, or *Noseweek* and cartoonists like Doonesbury perform exactly the same function.) Sociologists call this activity *debunking*.

And this somewhat grubby, less presentable side of society is to be found, not only in large corporations, but also in smaller ones, and in private lives. For example, students who present themselves in a sociology lecture each have a private room strewn with dirty clothes, bits of paper, half-finished bits of food, piles of books. Very many would be just a little embarrassed if someone were to see this 'unprepared' side of themselves. By the same token, restaurants also have a public space in which high standards of neatness, hygiene, politeness and efficiency are maintained. Behind the swing door into the kitchen these high standards often slip. (We all know stories of waiters who secretly spit in the soup in irritation at difficult patrons!)

So far in this chapter, I have argued that the sociological imagination does a number of interesting things to our way of seeing society. It puts things into a historical and cross-cultural perspective, which makes it difficult for us to believe that the way we do things is unique and absolute. It shows how things connect up in ways we had not thought of before, into broader and wider systems. One of these is the central connection between the law-abiding and law-breaking parts of society. And it punctures the way in which individuals and groups present themselves to society.

What is this thing called a 'society'? For sociologists a society is a group of people who have some internal sense of belonging and a discernible boundary between themselves and other groups. It is important that this boundary is a social rather than a physical one. It might be a language boundary, a historical sense of identity, or a cultural sense of togetherness. In the modern age it has often been assumed that a society is invariably the same thing as a nation-state. However, today national boundaries are fast being overshadowed by processes of globalization. So, a society could be a smaller unit like a tribe, a cultural minority group, a larger one like a nation-state, or it could be the 'global village'.

Are we free, or does society determine us?

As we have seen, one of the central perspectives of the sociological imagination is how social phenomena connect up into wider systems. That brings us to arguably the most persistent and abiding concern in all of sociology: the relationship between individual and society (also known as agent and structure). It is an issue that has occupied the minds of sociologists since the early nineteenth century. It is important partly because it touches on the universal issue of human freedom and determinism (that is, the extent to which we as human beings determine and choose our fate, or the extent to which it is determined for us). But it is important also because it defines more clearly than any other issue the contribution that sociology makes to the analysis of human society.

To answer the question of whether we are free of or determined by society, I will begin by showing how it is possible to argue that

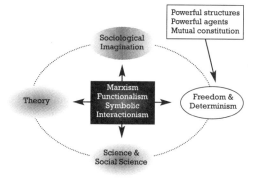

society governs our lives quite substantially. A central part of this argument is the sociological idea of structure. Then I will show how this argument is too one-sided, and that society cannot govern our lives completely. But, finally, I will argue that individuals cannot completely control either their own lives or the structures in which they are embedded. In more sociological language, structure and agency constitute each other.

The powerful influence of structures

Let us begin by considering the case of suicide. This is an extremely common phenomenon in modern society. It is quite likely that you will know someone in your immediate circle of family and friends who has either attempted suicide, has had serious thoughts about it, or has actually succeeded in killing themselves. And the reasons for this depressing activity are, most typically, matters of the heart, or of money. People kill themselves, or plan to, most often because of troubles in their relationships, or in their financial affairs.

Now, here is the intriguing part: Does this give us an idea of the causes of suicide, knowing people's reasons? Would a sociological theory of suicide concern itself with relationships and with finances? There is a range of sociologists, starting back in the nineteenth century with Emile Durkheim, who would say, no. Personal problems of this kind tell us very little about the roots of this phenomenon. The place to look for these roots is not in the reasons people give but rather in the broader patterns of society in which people are embedded. Durkheim said that it is primarily a person's religion, their marital status, and their place of residence, which determines whether or not they will commit suicide. So, if someone (in nineteenth-century France) were Jewish, married and living in a rural area, they would be quite unlikely to commit suicide. Conversely, they would be much more likely to do it if they were Protestant, unmarried and living in a city. (We will be discussing Emile Durkheim and his sociology in more detail in Chapter 3.)

And this line of thought still holds true for how sociologists understand suicide rates today. They say that we get a far better indication of people's tendency to commit suicide by investigating these wider, *structural* aspects of religion, marital status and place of residence, than by asking them about the state of their finances or of their relationships. Contrary to what almost everybody says, suicide is not about sexual partners or about money. This conclusion led Durkheim to be very sceptical about how much people know about themselves. For him, the average person has very little knowledge of or control over his or her own fate. People are influenced and governed by patterns that they have very little awareness of.

Think of the global spread of computers and the way this has changed people's lives. Buying a computer is one thing; keeping control over how children's tastes in entertainment then shift, almost inexorably, is quite another. (Parents who have tried to control the amount of time their children spend in front of computer or TV screens, know just how impossible it is to stem this tide.)

The consequence of this is that there is a most influential group of sociologists who would say that individuals have very little choice in running their own lives, that social structures are enormously influential, or in sociological terminology, that structure determines agency rather than vice versa. And it is unlikely that individuals can ever understand all of the ways in which this happens. The conclusion to be drawn from this is that to a large extent society operates quite independently of our control. It is almost as if we were all on a great ship sailing in the sea. And this ship takes us along with it, irrespective of our feverish activities on board.

What is a structure?

Until now we have been using the word 'structure' without defining it in detail. What is a structure? In sociology, a structure, very simply, is a regular pattern of behaviour in society. Structures are the grooves of accustomed, habituated activity into which people's lives fit. We can speak of family structures, racial structures, power structures, class structures, authority structures. Structures are the more fixed and inflexible parts of society. And they are fixed and inflexible because they are bolstered by religious or moral beliefs, by material interests, by

rewards and punishments, and so on. It is part of the fascination of sociology to unravel how structures take hold of people's lives, and how, without realizing it, individuals become subjected to their power.

For example, imagine a community that lives on the edge of a very wide plain with thick high grass. One day a brave individual finds a way across the plain through the grass, past all the dangerous wild animals. Other people follow this lead, and what used to be a thin, barely visible trail becomes a well-defined path which people use every day. Over time stories grow about the terrible things that happen to people who deviate from the path. And so no one ever leaves the path. Over generations the legend grows of the first heroic endeavour which pioneered the path over the plain.

At some stage, a powerful individual in the community gets to control the path, and charges a fee for anyone wishing to use it. He sees to it that laws are passed which punish anyone who strays from the path. Members from other communities are not permitted to use the path, since they are from a less privileged class. And so we could go on. The fixed path in this story, which over time becomes fixed in ever more subtle and ever more powerful ways, is an analogy (and an example) of how structures in society work and change over time.

Now, very few sociologists today would doubt the quite massive and hidden influence of structure in our lives. What they would question is the degree of choice we have.

Structures are not all-powerful

Let us consider this question: Can we say that we are merely passengers on a great societal ship that no one really steers or controls, where our own decisions count for nothing? No, that is not true.

First of all, society would not exist if there were no people. If society is 'doing' something, it can only be as a result of what its members are doing. It is only when individuals decide to commit suicide that there can be a suicide rate. (And the reason why religion, marital status and place of residence are important in suicide rates is because they provide people who are in trouble with support and comfort. Someone who is in trouble is less likely to commit suicide if he or she has someone to talk to: a wife, a priest, a family member.) It is only when individual people act as sons or daughters that families can exist. It is only when students sit in lectures that a university can exist.

Secondly, institutions like the family or the university gain power over individuals when they (the individuals) think of them in particular ways. We can see this happening when people talk about 'tradition' or 'custom' or 'history' as principles that bind them. They would say, 'We cannot change this practice because it is part of our tradition or our custom.' Sometimes they talk in similar terms about religion: 'I cannot do this because my religion forbids it.' Or more strongly, 'That's disgusting. I could never do that!' In each of these cases a prohibition has gained power by being detached from the people who initiated it. It is as if the prohibition has acquired a life of its own, quite separate from people. In these situations people are denying themselves the possibility of choice. Sociologists call this *reification*, the way in which social phenomena gain 'thing-like' status, as if human beings have nothing to do with their continued survival and power. (Reification means, quite literally, to make something into a thing.) It is exactly in this way that the path in our example above 'hardened' into an institution, a religion, a myth and an ideology.

Thirdly, people misunderstand how society works. They will say, for example, 'The real cause of underdevelopment among Africans is the huge population growth rate. Families are just too big. Get people to cut down on the number of children they have, and economic growth will follow.' The fact is that this link between population growth and economic development actually goes the other way round. We know today that when people's income and their education levels rise, their family sizes shrink, not vice versa. But a great many people continue to act on the erroneous belief that poverty is caused by family size. In this way, they disempower themselves. Their actions can have no effect whatsoever on the social structures around them. On the contrary, in some cases, their actions strengthen the result they are trying to avoid.

Imagine how the group of people living on the edge of the grass plain that we discussed earlier (on page 10) might start to change their path. Imagine what it would take for them to shift this structure, to challenge the powerful individuals in their society, to challenge the inbred beliefs and fears that have grown up around it, to rethink how the path might best wind its way across the plain. If you do this, you will of course be practising the sociological imagination.

In sum, there are three ways in which we can see that social structures are not independent of individual action and decisions. Structures depend for their existence on people. People have particular (reifying) attitudes to society, which undermine their freedom to make choices. And people have misconceptions about how society works.

These attitudes and misconceptions can, and frequently do, change. People think about themselves and their society. They write newspaper articles and books about their own society. They debate their own society in parliament or the equivalent of it wherever they are. They reflect on and puzzle over what is happening around them. They come to see things in a different light. Structures only exist and persist because individual people continue in the same way as they did the day before. Structures are recreated by our actions and decisions every day. And there are many reasons why people will make different decisions from one day to the next.

Can we ever be free?

Even though we as members of society make up and change structures, there is no way that we could ever have complete freedom of choice. There are three main reasons for this. Firstly, societies, especially large societies, are very complex entities. They have a multitude of cross-cutting groupings, power-nodes, lines of influence. It is virtually inconceivable that all of these movements, all of them in continual processes of change, could be perfectly understood and controlled. And that is what you would need to do to have total control over your own situation.

Secondly, the actions of human beings are driven by both the conscious and the unconscious. The conscious, rational drives are easier to grasp and guide. The unconscious impulses are in large measure unknowable. To the extent that social actions and the structures built on them are unconscious, unknowable and unfathomable, human beings will never be free of hidden influences.

Thirdly, and most importantly, just as structures depend on human individuals for their existence, so humans depend on structures for their existence. Human beings cannot exist outside of societal structures. This is true in a very literal sense. We know how deeply damaged children are who grow up in complete isolation from human interaction, or in cases where they had been reared by animals. In these cases children have been emotionally disturbed, they have been unable to speak or perform the most elementary physical tasks, they have been unable to walk or use simple tools. Teenagers have had the emotional age of two-year-olds. In short, we can say that human beings would hardly be human if society did not make them that.

We can understand this in another way if we think about our use of language. If we were unable to speak, our lives would be immeasurably impoverished. But in order to speak we need to subject ourselves to the structures and rules of language. We need to observe the rules of grammar and meaning to make ourselves understood. And frequently the more closely we follow these rules, that is, the more disciplined we are, the better we are able to express ourselves. To write poetry requires considerable application, but at the same time opens up new opportunities for self-expression. Playing the piano would not be possible without disciplined practice. Put differently, for our social existence, we depend completely on absorbing social structures, making them part of ourselves and of our bodies. As social beings we could not exist without structures, nor could social structures exist without us. In sociological terms, we say structures and agents are *mutually constitutive*. They make each other.

It is important to note, however, that agents are made in quite a different way from the way that social structures are made – certain structures enter into human beings in deep, subtle and quite unconscious ways. Consider the things that people eat in different parts of the world. Some might consider snake meat, sheep eyes, dog meat or frog legs to be delicacies, while others might be nauseated by the idea. The interesting part is that these latter beings with the 'delicate' constitutions do not choose to feel sick or even to vomit; their bodies choose for them. The rules and the taboos of their own society have sunk into them so deeply that they no longer have any control over their responses. That is why we say that people *internalize* the norms and values of society. It is as if what people have taken on board from outside of themselves has become an inseparable part of them.

The process by which human beings become part of their societies is called *socialization*. Individuals quite literally become social. Socialization does not happen exclusively by way of internalization. Certain social rules and practices are followed not because people agree with them but because they are afraid of the consequences of non-performance. All societies have rewards and punishments that accompany performance or non-performance of certain acts. But it is also probable that once these positive and negative sanctions have been in place for long enough, or if they have been applied early enough in a child's life, they will eventually become internalized. From this point of view, it is easy to see how powerful the influence of structures can be. For small children, for example, the world of their parents is the only world that exists for them. They have absolutely no defence against that world. For them it is not a question of choice between alternatives. Their parents' world is the only possible world. In this case, the influence of structure is virtually unstoppable. (We will return to the matter of socialization, and more particularly, the formation of the self when we discuss George Herbert Mead in Chapter 4.)

What is an agent?

Earlier we took time to define the term 'structures'. It is time we did the same for agents. What is an *agent* or *actor* in society? When you look at yourself and think what you are from day to day, you might say, 'I stay more or less constant from day to day. I have a permanent, unchanging core in me that carries me from situation to situation. If I am Lindiwe today, I will be Lindiwe tomorrow. I will be Lindiwe at school, and I will be Lindiwe at home. What's the problem? In addition, I take decisions about my own life. If I want something, I go out and get it. If I want to change my life, I just do it.'

There was a time when sociologists used to think the same way about individuals. However, today we consider individual people to be much more complicated. They are made up of quite different parts. The way you act and speak in the presence of your parents is quite different from the way you act when you are with your friends. Your behaviour in front of a priest is not quite what it would be at a rave party. This is why sociologists speak of a *decentred self*, one which has no constant fixed centre.

In addition, as I mentioned earlier, a large part of us is made up of the unconscious. Many of the things we do come from quite misty places deep down inside us, places that are extremely difficult to understand and change. They are difficult to understand because they are guarded by strong emotions, like anxiety, disgust, anger, and fear. And it is those dark, misty and frightening places that society's structures have entered, becoming part of us, long before we were aware of it.

In other words, sociologists today do not think of individuals in society as independent and self-determined decision-makers with a constant fixed core. Rather, they see human beings as a collection of quite disparate bits, substantially influenced by unconscious and hidden urges and also by the structures of society. This does not mean that they are nothing more than puppets under the control of social structures. People reflect on themselves, change their minds, their attitudes, their knowledge, and so they change society around them, albeit in limited ways.

So, what have we been saying up to now about the interplay of agents and structures? First of all, we have said that social structures operate to a significant degree beyond the control of individuals in society. However, and secondly, this does not mean that structures can exist independently of individual action. Structures would not exist without human action. And social actors often attribute more power to structures than is warranted, that is, they reify structures. At times, people do not understand how structures work, and that also increases the influence of structures. In both these last two cases, things might easily

change, and people could gain significant control over their lives. But, thirdly, individuals can never gain complete control over their lives or over the society which governs their lives. Societies are too complex for that. And many of the influences over individual action are unconscious, and therefore unknowable. But, crucially, structures constitute agents and make them what they are. In the end, structures and agents are mutually constitutive. Neither one can exist or operate without the other.

Science, social science and common sense: Is sociology scientific?

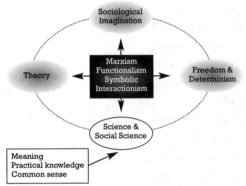

In the nineteenth century, Auguste Comte, one of the very first sociologists, constructed a historical theory of human society and human thought. In this theory Comte saw in human society a gradually evolving progression over time through three phases, from (i) theological thinking, to (ii) metaphysical thinking, to (iii) 'positivistic' or scientific thinking. This he called the Law of the Three Stages.

Theological thinking, according to Comte, explained the way the world worked by reference to supernatural beings and spirits. But it did this with a minimum of factual evidence. Over time, theological thinking was replaced with metaphysical thinking. This form of thought rejected theological thinking. In contrast, it explained things by reference to the essences of phenomena, like the inner nature of human beings.

The coming of the modern age, the so-called Enlightenment, was marked by scientific thinking. For Comte, this was the most advanced of the three stages. It rejected reference to supernatural beings and to essences. It was based on factual observation and experimentation. Within the realm of scientific thinking, sociology was the most advanced since it was the most complex. Although it was the youngest discipline, it relied on and went beyond all the other disciplines. And, for its strength, it relied on the same principles as the other sciences.

Comte contributed strongly to an ongoing and central debate in sociology, namely, whether society can be studied in the same way as natural phenomena, like gravity, and whether sociological theory is of the same kind as natural science theory. Comte was a positivist in the modern sense of the word. He thought that society could indeed be studied in the same way as natural phenomena, and that sociological theory could enjoy the same stature and validity as natural science theory.

In the following section we will see why Comte was wrong. Unlike natural science, sociology is built on the analysis of meaning. Sociologists have to talk to people in order to understand how they understand the world. However, people cannot tell you everything they know because part of their knowledge is practical knowledge that cannot be put into words. Social science does share one important aspect with natural science, and that is that it is responsible knowledge. It does not build its conclusions on gossip, or on divine revelation, or on metaphysical assumptions. Social science is built on empirical observation.

The importance of meaning

Whichever way you argue, and today there is still a great deal of such argument, we have to take into account that social phenomena differ in one crucial way from natural phenomena, and that is that social phenomena are based on the construction of meaning. Members of society interact with each other on the basis of meaning and of symbolic exchanges, the most important of which is language. In addition, members of society have their own theories or suppositions on how society works, they have a so-called *common sense* idea of what society is about.

This entails two important principles for sociological investigation and for sociological theory. Firstly, in order to study society, sociologists must invariably speak to people. Secondly, in order to construct sociological theory sociologists must build on lay people's common sense theories.

The contrast between natural science and science could not be more stark. Natural scientists do not – in fact, cannot – talk to the atoms or rocks or plants that they study. It follows that they would not even conceive of asking these

Auguste Comte, who lived in early nineteenth-century France (1798-1857), is often regarded as the original father of sociology, mainly because he first introduced the word sociology – an uncomfortable mix of Latin (socius = companion) and Greek (logos = of reason). He regarded sociology as the 'queen of the sciences'. He is famous for his Law of the Three Stages – theological, metaphysical and scientific thinking – which we discussed earlier in this section.

objects how they work. However, social scientists could not do their work without doing just that.

The critical importance of meaning can be clearly illustrated in the case of so-called stimulus-response reactions. When someone gets jabbed by a sharp object, you might expect them to jump automatically, even get angry – an automatic, unthinking response to a (painful) stimulus. And you could say that this was a natural reaction, just as predictable as the way in which gravity works. However, the randomness of this 'natural reaction' is easily shown, because people do not always respond in the same way to 'sharp jabs'. It depends crucially on whether they *interpret* that sharp jab to be a thorn, a syringe needle, a scorpion sting, a sewing needle or possibly something else. And from their interpretation would flow very different emotions: irritation, fear, helplessness, or just not much at all.

The important point is that it all depends on the *meaning* which people attribute to the jab. There is no such thing as an *automatic* and predictable response to a sharp jab, as there might be an automatic and predictable consequence when I allow an object to drop to the ground. The law of gravity does not rely on interpretation or meaning. When, as a sociologist, I study people's responses, I have to start by asking how they experience things, and how they understand things. In more technical terms, we would say that human behaviour is mediated by meaning.

Practical knowledge

If we all have one kind of knowledge called common sense that sociologists use in constructing their theories, there is a second kind, called *practical knowledge*, which has equally intriguing implications for sociological theory. Here I am referring to skills like being able to ride a bicycle or knock in a nail with a hammer. We all know that you can't explain to someone how to ride a bicycle and then expect them to be able to do it straightaway. In most cases, they will need to practise, and even with a great deal of help from you, it will take them some time to get the hang of it. They will fall over a few times, make a whole lot of mistakes (probably blame you for being a bad instructor),

but eventually succeed in carrying on (in a wobbly fashion) on their own. In this situation, we would say, there is no theory of bicycle-riding. What we mean is that the skill cannot be expressed in words. It cannot be articulated. It is as if this peculiar 'knowledge' lodges in our muscles, and once we have acquired it, we seldom forget.

This has an interesting implication. When you talk to people, they cannot necessarily tell you everything they know, even if you ask them quite explicitly. For example, a master cabinet-maker can tell you some things about the craft of cabinet-making, but you will not be able to acquire that knowledge unless you spend some years 'doing' the craft. There is a whole lot of knowledge that our bodies 'know' but that we cannot express in language. This applies to a staggering range of activities in our lives, from carrying on a coherent conversation, to writing with a pen, or typing on a keyboard, or eating with a knife and fork, or walking across a room (think, for example, how long it takes babies to learn to walk).

So, to conclude what we have been saying, social science is different from natural science because it (social science) is built on the communication of meaning, and the communication of theories of how society works. Secondly, unlike atoms and apples and rocks, people *know* things, but they know these things in very different ways. Some of this knowledge can be expressed; some cannot. But, thirdly (and as we will see in the following section), social science is not the same as common sense.

Sociology is more than common sense

Sociology is often criticized for saying some very obvious and banal things, things that everyone already knows – like, for example, racism is caused by situations of conflict. Is sociology then little more than pretentious common sense dressed up in fancy jargon?

I have explained that sociology is necessarily built on common sense, which is where all sociological investigation must start. But it does not stop there. Sociology goes beyond common sense because it tests its evidence and its argument.

For example, when my great aunt Muriel rolls her eyes heavenward and exclaims, 'Really, my dear, the youth of today are completely undisciplined!', I do not ask her how many of the so-called 'youth' she has interviewed, what her criteria for judging 'undisciplined' are, whether this is true of only 1999 or of 1998 and 1938 (which is about when she herself was a 'youth') as well. But those are some of the things which sociologists might do in considering Aunt Muriel's statement. In this sense sociological investigation, like all science, is a responsible activity. It answers to public criteria of accountability. It publishes its results in journals and books where they can be checked and questioned by other sociologists. It also makes its sources known so that others can verify them. That points to the practice of referencing. When you write an essay you will be required to reference all your sources. This is time-consuming and often tedious. But it is necessary because this is how we participate in the publicly accountable language of science.

If we were less than kind to my great aunt Muriel, we would say that she was basing her opinions on hearsay and gossip. She has picked up her information from her friends (around the tea table) and not from talking to the very 'youth' she accused of being undisciplined. In sociological terms, she lacks empirical support for her theories. Sociology, then, is different from gossip, because gossip does not conform to our rules of responsible language.

But think back for a moment to August Comte, and his ideas about religious thinking and metaphysical thinking. Religious thinkers might say, in this instance, that, according to 'the holy book' (I am using a completely imaginary holy book, of course), young people are different from adults and that they (young people) need to be disciplined. Note that religious thinking is coming to the same conclusion as my great aunt Muriel, but by means of using divine authority, that is, the holy book or the prophet. Again there is no foundation in factual research.

Metaphysical thinkers, by contrast, might say that human beings, in essence, are good. But this goodness takes time to develop in their lives, and such development needs education and discipline. In this case, too, we have an argument based on equally unfactual and axiomatic suppositions. There is no foundation in empirical research, although metaphysical thinkers (or philosophers, as they would be called today) would be very concerned about the precision and the logic of their thinking.

So, as a social science, sociology relies on common sense, builds on it and goes further than it. That makes sociology a shaky science because people can, and do, change their minds about themselves, and that changes the sociological theory built on their opinions. But sociology goes beyond common sense because it uses scientific criteria to judge itself, and it is based on factual research. This makes sociology, as a social science, different from gossip, and from religious thinking, and from metaphysical thinking.

Question

When you read a story in a newspaper, would you say it is based on hard science, gossip, or revelation? After all, we all read newspaper articles with a pinch of salt. And how about the 'facts' that you read about in advertisements?

What is theory?

There are many uses of the word 'theory' in the English language. For instance, when you have a detective investigating a murder case, and he has a *suspicion* of who committed the crime, he might say, 'I don't really know who killed Mr B, but I have a theory.' Or he might say, 'Nobody has any facts about this case. It is all purely theoretical.' What he means to say is that it is all *speculation*. But if he is a good detective, he will gather together the clues and the evidence, keep comparing them with his suspicion (something like a picture in his head), and over time his suspicion of who had done it will harden into firm knowledge. From his 'firm knowledge' he will be able to make predictions that link the butler to the poison in the wineglass, and amaze the people around him. (In detective stories, the investigator hero is always surrounded by particularly slow and dim-witted people.)

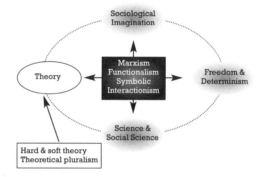

However, when sociologists use the term *theory*, they do not mean suspicion or speculation. They mean something close to our Sherlock Holmes's 'firm knowledge'. More specifically, they mean a systematized body of thinking that explains how society works or how its parts hang together. So, functionalist

21

theory, for example, explains how the various parts of society (education, the family, politics, culture, production) are linked to each other, and how they contribute to the functioning of society as a whole. It is *systematized* because all the theory's concepts are related to one another in logical ways. And it is a body of *thinking* because it is like a mental picture we carry in our heads which is supposed to correspond more or less to the reality outside of our heads. It is the purpose of science (that is, the responsible language we discussed earlier) to keep testing that the correspondence or match between the 'picture' and the 'reality' is as close as possible.

In the following sections I will distinguish between 'hard' and 'soft' theory, and discuss the problem of theoretical pluralism, that is, what happens when you have more than one theory that can be used to explain a phenomenon.

Hard theory and soft theory

Hard theory, also called positivist theory, indicates a language that explains the world around us in terms of causes and results. In this kind of language we would typically say, 'When A occurs, we expect B to occur', or more simply, 'A causes B.' There is quite a firm link between cause and result. So, for example, we would say, as we have said earlier, 'When individuals are under stress and they have no one to talk to, they commit suicide.' The implication of such reasoning is that, whenever we find people who show these attributes, we can *predict* that they will act in a particular way.

And that means, quite dramatically, that we can intervene in time to stop it from happening or we can change the way it happens. It is like finding the cause of a disease: once you know what causes the disease, you can devise strategies or policies to prevent it spreading. Likewise, in society, if we knew the cause of racism, we could develop effective anti-racist policies.

Hard theories are also usually macro-theories. That means that they deal with the broad and big issues of society, like class divisions, or the population growth rate, or how economics interact with education, and how politics interact with culture and ideology. Examples of hard macro-theories are functionalism and Marxism, two theories we will be discussing in Chapters 2 and 3 respectively.

Hard theory, or positivism, has, however, been subjected to a great deal of criticism. Few social scientists today would be so brave as to say that they can predict what is going to happen in society. In fact, the whole notion of causation is problematic when you are dealing with human beings who communicate through meaning. As you will remember, the interpretation of meaning is quite a tricky business. In reaction to these criticisms of hard theory sociologists have developed soft theory.

Soft theorists do not think that human relations can be explained in terms of causes and results. For this kind of theory, the main task is *understanding*, not explaining. Social relationships are based on the exchange of meaning and symbols. It is notoriously difficult to be precise about meaning. Meaning tends to slip and slide from situation to situation. And because symbols have roots in the unconscious, it can take quite a bit of digging to get to the bottom of meaning. On this basis, it is impossible to talk about causes and effects. The very same thing can elicit dramatically different responses from different people, or even from the same person in different situations. Remember how differently people can respond to a sharp prick.

If the possibilities for explanation are undermined here, it follows that the possibilities for prediction and policy will also be doubtful. For this kind of theory, things (even quite 'factual' things) are much more tentative, uncertain, and given to dispute. It is also very difficult to build statements into systemic patterns of theory.

On the other hand, even if it cannot make hard causal statements, this kind of theory listens much more carefully to what people are saying, and what their (multiple) meanings are. In many cases this kind of theory has been strongly influenced by psychological and especially Freudian theory. This means that they have developed techniques for very detailed and careful analysis of both conscious and unconscious aspects of human meaning.

That means that soft theories are also usually micro-theories. They focus on small-scale situations, between very few individuals, like the way in which individuals formulate their racial identities, or the flow of a conversation between a teacher and the pupils. Examples of soft theory in sociology are *symbolic interactionism, ethnomethodology,* and *hermeneutics,* as shown in the following table.

THEORY	
Macro-theory	**Micro-theory**
Functionalism	Symbolic interactionism
Marxism	Ethnomethodology
	Hermeneutics

Theoretical pluralism

It is an attribute of sociological theorizing that, in any one topic, there could be, and often is, more than one theory being applied. Thus, there are both functionalist and Marxist macro-theories of education. And there is also a symbolic interactionist micro-theory of education. That could be confusing because we are accustomed to having one truth in a situation. It was either the butler who killed Mr B or it wasn't. In the courts, there might be a great deal of argument and evidence one way or another, but ultimately someone is either guilty or innocent. You can't have it both ways.

But sociology does try to have it both ways — or, to put it more precisely, it is usually a whole lot more difficult to make a decision one way or another. There are a number of reasons for this. Firstly, the social world contains a huge amount of evidence. If you select or emphasize one set of facts, you say one thing. If you choose another set, you say something else. Think about your own lifetime biography and how many hours it would take for a researcher to get to know everything about you. Any number of theories could be possible depending on which set of facts you choose to focus on.

Secondly, the social world changes from place to place. In one place, one set of rules might apply, and in another place another set of rules. You would need different theories to talk about those different places.

Thirdly, social researchers are human beings with their own prejudices and biases. Their personal make-ups incline them to accept one kind of theory and not another. (Some people don't like being tentative. They prefer theories that give them firm and strong answers. So, they would not approve of soft theory.)

Whatever the reason, when you read sociology you will often find more than one theory competing in the same area. That can be confusing. How do we deal with this situation? Some writers take an *eclectic* position. For them there is no correct and exhaustive theory. Sociologists should have at their disposal a range of theories to draw from, they say, a different one for each different situation. Like a mechanic with a different size spanner for each different nut in the car engine. So, for macro-situations you would use macro-theories, and for micro-situations you would use micro-theories.

That solution to the problem is, however, difficult, because most macro-theories have a clear explanation for micro-situations. Marxists, for example, often follow Karl Marx's famous principle: 'Men make their own history but not in conditions of their own choosing.' In other words, individuals do have the freedom to choose, but this is a limited and constrained freedom. Marx is saying that ultimately structures are more influential than agents. So, an eclectic position would be contradictory here if it tried to bring in a micro-theory to explain micro-situations for Marxism, because Marxism already has such a theory.

Other writers argue that you cannot make a final choice between theories. Each theory offers a perspective on social reality that does not exclude other perspectives. So, it is not a case of one theory being superior to another, but a case of each theory offering insights and lines of investigation that the other does not. Thus, for example, Marxist theory, as we shall see in Chapter 2, looks for instances of power domination and conflict between groups in society where other theories would be silent. By contrast, functionalist theory would be sensitive to dimensions of integration and coherence in society that Marxism would ignore.

Yet others argue that the great sociological writers like Karl Marx and Max Weber presented sophisticated and extremely subtle insights into the human condition. They worked with a rare sensitivity to how members of society behave and how their various actions cohere. In this sense sociologists are like artists, and their work quite like literature. We can return to their work again and again, seeing new perspectives and new angles at each reading. Here, too, it would be extremely difficult to choose one writer above another.

In the end, and for the various reasons discussed here, many sociologists today would not choose one theory above another. That has a difficult implication, though, because it means that you have to know more than one theory. That means knowing all its various concepts and principles, and being able to apply them in particular situations or to particular problems, which entails a whole lot more work.

In Chapters 2, 3 and 4 of this book, we will be looking at three particular theories: Marxism, functionalism and symbolic interactionism. The first two are macro-theories and the last is a micro-theory. In many ways therefore they are complementary perspectives. We will see how particular sociological writers work with the big issues that we have been discussing. Each writer has a particular take on questions like the relationship between individual and society, or how society fits together and integrates.

You will also see how sociologists can be magicians opening up new and unexpected aspects of the world to us, or system-builders linking disparate elements into larger and intricate patterns, or scientists pinning down their findings with hard evidence and clear logic, or even artists who understand human beings in subtle and quite intuitive ways.

2 Marxism

Marxism is unusual among modern sociological theories because it retains a close connection and identification with its founder, Karl Marx. It says a great deal for the brilliance, the intellectual power and the influence of Marx that he is still taken so seriously.

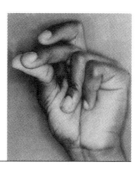

However, Marx is taken seriously, very seriously and rather humourlessly, for another reason, too.

This is because he is closely connected to the rise of communism. That fact elicits strong emotions from people despite the collapse of the Soviet Union in 1989. On the one hand, Marx is seen as the arch-enemy of the free market system and a lethal threat to the Western way of life. On the other hand, Marxism is regarded as the friend of the workers, the only means of protection against exploitative bosses.

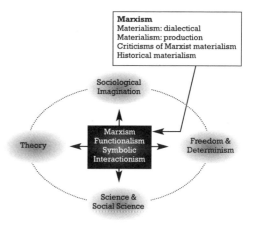

Unfortunately both of these views bring far too much heat and far too much politics into what concerns us here. For our purposes Marx is a writer of profound sociological importance and, as we shall see, a rich source of insights concerning both societies, in general, and modern society, in particular. The political slogans that supposedly derive from his work often do considerable violence to his principles.

A great deal of Marxist theory rests on a proper understanding of the term *materialism*, and the terms associated with it,

Karl Marx was born in 1818 in the German town of Trier, and died in London in 1883. Marx was forced to move to London after he had made himself extremely unpopular with the governments of France, Germany and Belgium. He lived in extreme poverty for most of his life until Friederich Engels made provision for him. His major works included *Capital* (3 volumes: 1867, 1885, 1894), *The Communist Manifesto* (1848), and *The German Ideology* (1845).

like *historical materialism* and *dialectical materialism*. This is complicated by the fact that materialism can mean two different things. It can refer to how individuals are determined and changed by society and how society is changed by individuals. It can also indicate the fundamental importance of production activities in societies. Marxists say that knowledge of the productive foundation of society tells us a great deal about other aspects of society. Historical materialism is Marx's theory of history, that is, how societies change from one form to another. Let us look at these ideas in more detail.

Materialism: the spiral of change

The term *materialism* has a number of closely related meanings. The first and most important concerns the relationship between the individual and society. In this first sense, materialism means that members of society are, for all practical purposes, shaped and determined by their social circumstances. In the second meaning of the word, production is seen as a powerful influence on other parts of society.

Let us consider the first meaning, namely that society determines the individual. There is, for Marx, no human essence that escapes society's influence. We are not born with a 'pre-social' element which resists society's shaping. The eighteenth-century French philosopher Jean Jacques Rousseau famously wrote about the 'noble savage'. By this he meant that people are born good but are corrupted by civilization. In the same vein, many people today believe fervently that 'essentially', or 'deep down' or 'in our heart of hearts' we are born good. Others, quite predictably, and equally fervently, think we are born bad or 'basically evil'.

For Marx, this is essentialist thinking and he will have none of it. Human beings do not have inborn and unchangeable essences. We are completely shaped by the conditions in which we grow up. What we believe, the way we behave, are all socially determined.

It follows from this principle, for example, that the drive to make money in modern capitalism is not a universal characteristic of human existence. There are numerous examples in history of societies where the urge to accumulate wealth was not a prime social value. For Marx, the restless drive for profit, and for continual reinvestment is a product of a particular society at a particular time in history. If it is not part of human essence, if there is no such thing as human essence, then the profit motive can change, can disappear, can become its very opposite.

You may be thinking by now that Marx pictured human beings simply as puppets of the broader society in which they live, moulded and shaped any which way. But here's a slight complication: for Marx, human beings also have the capacity to create things, to make their ideas happen. To put this differently, what is inside our heads can become a material reality outside of us. And this is just as true of concrete objects that we make or shape, say, from wood or rock, as it is of social institutions like schools or families. Members of society can create tools and they can create social institutions. More importantly, those institutions can then become part of the social environment in which they live. In other words, we can shape the conditions which, in their turn, shape us.

Now, all of us grow up in societies that have already been created by those before us. We are primarily shaped by conditions that have been given to us by our predecessors and our ancestors. We can, as we have seen, shift and change what has been passed down to us, but we have to start this process from the historical place where we happen to find ourselves. Or, to put this differently, we can change and shape the social conditions in which we find ourselves, but we do it in a way that is influenced by those conditions. Consider what happens when the government of a country wants to change the schooling system. Given the time and the resources, they can do this quite easily. But the way they do it will be deeply influenced by the fact that they were all educated by that same schooling system. Marx expresses this same principle as follows:

> Men make their own history but not in circumstances
> of their own choosing.

What we have said so far is this. Step one, members of society are deeply influenced by the circumstances in which they grow up. Step two, members of society can also influence those very same circumstances (although these circumstances also shape the way they might think about changing things). Now let us go on to a third step.

Once we have changed our social circumstances, they influence us in a different way from the way they did before. And when we think about changing them, we will, in turn, not think about changing them in the way we did before, because we will have different ideas and resources at our disposal.

Consider our example of the schooling system. A government may have changed the country's schooling system in the year 1960. Those changes may have been efficiently or inefficiently implemented, and the results will almost certainly not be what the government expected. In 1972 they may again consider changes, but the changes they now consider will be profoundly influenced by the 1960 changes, and how these (unintentionally) turned out.

What we have here is an example of Marx's dialectic, and more specifically, his *dialectical materialism*. Two elements – the individual and society – are in interaction. They mutually influence each other, and by this process set up a spiral of continual change, as shown in the following diagram. Starting from the bottom, each circle of the spiral produces an interaction between a changed society and a changed individual. That means that each interaction will be different too.

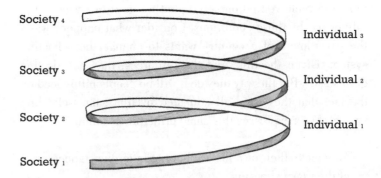

Society 4   Individual 3

Society 3   Individual 2

Society 2   Individual 1

Society 1

Materialism: production as the foundation of society

We shall see further on that Marx uses the term dialectic in a somewhat different context as well. But in order to get there we first need to consider another meaning of the word materialism.

In this sense, the term refers to the importance of production in society. For Marx, the activity of production is fundamental to any society since, without production, that is, the production of food, of shelter or of tools, no society would be able to exist. From this he deduces the principle that many of the other activities in society are significantly influenced by the particular process of production. Thus, when we refer to the Stone Age, the Iron Age, or the Bronze Age, we are referring to the tools that people used during those times. By using a tool to depict a whole age, we are acknowledging, as Marx did, the importance of the social processes which were made possible by the use of those (production) tools.

For Marx, then, once we understand how the production process works in society, we can deduce a whole lot about the way the rest of society works. It is as if the production process lays the foundation on which other parts of society are built. And like a house, there are a limited number of house shapes which can be built on any particular foundation. In the same way, the production system in any society will significantly determine what the government looks like, the nature of religion in society, and how educational systems work.

This is easier to understand when you see that, for Marx, the production process is closely linked to the major groupings or classes in society. Historically, the production processes associated with various kinds of society have always involved two major classes, a *ruling class* and a *subject class*. And these classes are always in conflict. We shall see in a moment that not all societies have these classes. But the point to make here is that the production process has a profound influence on the way other sectors of society operate.

Let us consider an example. The economy of ancient Rome was based on agriculture (growing grapes for wine, olives and wheat) and the labour force for these farms was made up of thousands of slaves. Most of these slaves were prisoners of war. The major classes in Roman society were, on the one hand, landowners, and on the other, slaves. The most important dynamic in Roman society was, predictably, the conflict between these two groups, the one demanding more and more efficient labour, the other resisting awful working and living conditions. A critical activity in this society was quite logically the conduct of war in which further prisoners, and therefore more slaves, were taken. And an important part of the way the landowning class thought about themselves was how different they were from 'savage, uncouth', foreign slaves, and reasons why slaves should not participate or vote in the government of Rome. This thinking was also reflected in the legal system, which laid out in some detail the rights and obligations of slaves, and the way they could, or could not, be treated. The ferocious punishment by public crucifixion was originally designed by Roman landowners to deter runaway slaves and suppress slave rebellions. This clearly shows how significantly the production process influenced other aspects of society.

According to Marxism, society is divided into two major parts: the *base* and *superstructure*. The base refers to the production system of society, whether it be capitalist or feudal. That includes the technology used in production and the technical know-how that goes with it. It also includes the division of society into conflicting classes. So, a slave society, like the Romans, has its own particular way of economic production, which is closely linked to the relationship between the ruling and subject classes.

If that is the base, then the superstructure refers to the remaining cultural, political and ideological aspects of society. So, when I said just now that 'the production process strongly influenced other aspects of society', I can translate this into more technical Marxist language by saying, the base determined the superstructure.

This second sense of materialism has some interesting implications, and they have to do with the notions of systematizing and debunking that we considered in Chapter 1. The first implication is that social elements cannot be seen in isolation from one other. They must be seen in relation to the totality of society, and more particularly in relation to the economic base. The second implication is that however people might present themselves or their institutions in public, there is frequently a different kind of reality hiding behind these presentations.

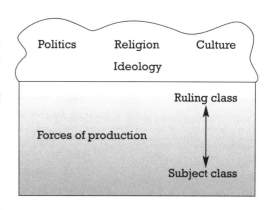

Let us take our example of the schooling system again. Schools as institutions do not exist separately from one another. They all form part of a broader system that is subjected to common policy principles, common behaviour and common ways of thinking. Likewise, the schooling system itself is related to other parts of society. Schools are designed to produce skilled workers for the labour market. They are significantly affected by the economic base of society.

But schools also present themselves in particular ways. Many people think that schools are a source of equality in society. They are, so they say, run on the basis of merit. Anyone has access to schooling. Anyone with intelligence and will can do well and come out on top.

But that is not quite true. In reality, schools often perpetuate the inequalities in society. Wealthy people's children tend to do better at school than poor people's children, and so land up with better jobs and higher wages. This is not because wealthy people intend it that way. Often it is quite unintended. Wealthy families give their children a whole range of educational advantages even before they enter the school gates. In their homes they will have radios, televisions, books and computers. All of these, quite unintentionally, prepare children for schooling and give them significant advantages over children from poorer families. In short, schools are often quite different from the way they are presented.

So far, then, we have discussed two meanings of the word materialism. In the first, members of society both shape and are shaped by, the social circumstances in which they grow up and live. In the second the economic base of society significantly determines the way in which the superstructure operates.

Criticisms of Marxist materialism

It is important to take note of the different words I am using to describe the influence of material circumstances. In the first, material conditions 'shape' and 'are shaped by' members of society. In the second, the base 'significantly determines' the superstructure. The difference between the two, signals areas of considerable debate within and around Marxism.

Let us consider the first. The way I have written it, in the interaction between individual and society, each is presented as having equal value. Individuals are presented as if they influence society as much as society influences them (although we have shown that it depends a great deal on the critical attitude or lack of it which individuals have towards society). In effect, the way Marx wrote about these principles shifted significantly during the course of his life. In the early part of his life he was much more concerned about the position of individuals and their opportunities for changing things. Later in life, when he became more interested in economics, he presented society much more as a giant machine that operated according to principles which individuals could not easily change. Marx is often then criticized for downplaying the role of individuals in shaping society. In technical terms, he is taken to task for being a *structural determinist*.

The second debate concerns the importance of the role of economics in society. Marxism has often been criticized for presenting society in too 'economistic' a way. In other words, so say the critiques, it has overemphasized the importance of economic factors and underplayed the role of culture, religion, politics, and the like.

You will remember that in describing the relationship between these parts of society, I used the metaphor of a house being built on a particular (economic) foundation. And I said that the shape of the house would be significantly limited by the original foundation layout. This metaphor already gives the economic base a preponderant influence in the shape of the house. Why, for example, is it economics that is presented as the foundation and not politics or culture? When people talk about the South Korean economic miracle, for example, they

often place enormous emphasis on culture to explain consistent and high rates of growth, the Confucian culture of hard work and obedience to authority. In this case, culture is being used to explain economics, and not vice versa. There is no obvious reason why culture cannot be as significant a social factor as economics.

Historical materialism

It is time to consider Marx's ideas on social change, or his theory of *historical materialism*. Earlier we spoke about the notion of dialectical materialism as the interaction of conflicting elements which leads to a spiral of change. At that point I used the individual and society as examples of these conflicting elements. Now I want to use classes in society – ruling class and subject class – as another example of this.

For Marx, unlike other writers, social change is not something that needs special explanation. The notion of dialectics, built as it is on the idea of conflicting elements (classes), assumes a state of constant spiralling change in society.

Where does conflict come from? In order to understand this we need to go back in history to what Marx termed 'communalistic' society or primitive communism. Today we would call these hunter-gatherer societies. Structurally, they are very simple societies. There is very little division of labour or hierarchy in this society. Most social structures are built around the extended family. What is important for our story is that they are subsistence societies. People have only enough to keep themselves going for very brief stretches of time. There is very little extra (or surplus) to go on. For Marx, this is the one society in history that is not structurally a conflictual one. There is no ruling class or subject class to speak of, no class conflict, and therefore very little ongoing change.

This relatively peaceful state of affairs changes when the hunter-gathering mode of production moves to one of settled agriculture, when improved technology allows farmers to produce more than they need in the short term. In other words, they begin to produce a *surplus*. At this point an accumulation

Marxism is a
remarkably neat and
logical theory. All the
various parts of
society fit into a
beautifully organized
pattern: economic
production, ruling and
subject classes,
ideology and culture,
historical change. But
consider now how it
does the things we
discussed earlier.
Does it debunk false
images in society?
Does it relativize ideas
that we might think are
unique to us? Does it
build connections
between elements in
society to make a
system? Is it hard
science or soft
science? How does it
address meaning?

of surplus by particular individuals becomes possible, and thus rising inequality between individuals. Out of such a situation in turn can arise a hierarchy of authority and the appearance of elementary forms of government (through chiefs and kings). It is from this point on, says Marx, that conflict between classes is a permanent feature of societies in history. Because some (few) accumulate wealth, and others (many) are pushed in one way or another to work for them.

Marx divides society into various major stages: primitive communism or communalism, ancient (slave) societies, feudalism, capitalism, socialism and communism. Slave societies, feudalism and capitalism are all marked by conflict between ruling and subject classes. In each case the conflict grows and intensifies until the point of revolution. At this point, society is restructured. The old polarity of conflict is replaced with a new one. New classes arise to replace the old ones. The dialectic moves up one level. And this sets in motion a new polarity leading to a new revolution, and new mode of production.

Marx's Stages of History

1 Primitive

2 Ancient (slave) societies

3 Feudalism

4 Capitalism

5 Socialism

6 Communism

Socialism, however, is the point at which the inequality between classes ceases. It is, in theory, no more the case that some (the subject class) work for others (the ruling class), or that some accumulate wealth at the expense of the others. It follows (again, in theory) that conflict will cease, and with it also the continuing spiral of change. This is why Marx talks of socialism (and its successor, communism) as the end of history. What he meant was that this is the end of change.

3 Functionalism

Alongside Marxism, functionalism is the second major stream of macro-theorizing in sociology. This means that, like Marxism, it lays more emphasis on the influence of society on the individual than the other way round. It concentrates on the broad structural features of society.

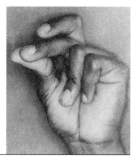

Functionalism and Marxism, therefore, overlap in a number of important ways. However, in many other ways, they are not only different but in conflict. That is because functionalism has been seen as a conservative social theory, which means that it has tried to depict society as harmonious and stable. In modern times it has also been linked to modernization theory, which has argued that industrial capitalism, in general, and American society, in particular, are the highpoint of social development.

Marxism, by contrast, has argued that most societies in human history are conflictual, unstable and given to revolution. Marxists have been stridently critical of industrial capitalism and have sought ways to undermine and replace it with alternative forms of society.

Whichever position you support, it is important to remember that functionalism and Marxism are theories that have been in energetic conversation with each other for more than a century and a half. They have criticized each other, attempted to outmanoeuvre each other intellectually, and even opposed each other politically. Already in the mid-nineteenth century, the first major author of functionalist theory, Emile Durkheim, spent a great deal of effort in discussing and criticizing Marx. In the late twentieth century, the other dominant functionalist figure, Talcott Parsons, also felt the need to consider Marx in some detail.

In our discussion of functionalism, then, we will consider first the writings of Durkheim, and then those of Parsons. We will be covering a number of key concepts both for functionalism and for sociological theory in general.

Emile Durkheim

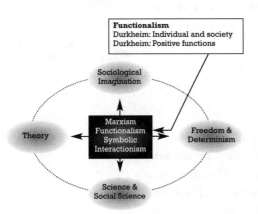

Functionalism
Durkheim: Individual and society
Durkheim: Positive functions

Sociological Imagination

Marxism Functionalism Symbolic Interactionism

Theory

Freedom & Determinism

Science & Social Science

In the first section on Durkheim I argue that, for functionalists, society has a massive and powerful influence on the individual. Society has an external existence to individuals and exercises telling constraint over their behaviour. In the second section I explain that, for functionalists, society hangs together because of a fundamental agreement on basic values among its members, a value consensus. In the third section I show that what is functionalist about functionalist argument is the emphasis on the positive benefits that flow from particular aspects of society for the system as a whole.

Individual and society

Much like Marx earlier on, Durkheim was scathing about those theorists who placed excessive emphasis on the individual. Today we would call them methodological individualists. For them all aspects of society must be explained first by reference to individual members of society. Also, they would say, individuals have a lot more influence on society than vice versa. (Further on we will see that this is exactly what Max Weber does.)

For Durkheim, however, society exhibits three prime characteristics, all of which indicate its priority over its members. These are 'externality', 'constraint' and 'emergence'. By *externality* he meant that society exists prior to our entry into it, and it will continue to exist after our departure from it. It is like temporarily being part of a flowing river. The river continues independently of our floating down in it for a while.

Externality also means that individuals are always part of a wider and broader social system. I am a son or brother or father by virtue of the fact that I am part of a bigger unit called a family. I am a sociology lecturer because I am part of a totality called a university. There is no part of me that does not have links with the structures of society around me.

In a 1999 film, *The Matrix*, a man comes to the nightmarish conclusion one day that his whole life, in fact everybody's lives, are simply expressions of a computer programme. Human beings are nothing more than creations of some software writer's fantasy. They exist in a computer-generated world. However, he comes to discover a resistance group who have managed to break out of this dream-world and work to liberate all humans from their captivity.

For Durkheim, and, in fact, for many sociologists today, we live in a socially constructed world, but, and here's the scary thing, there is no escape from it. Even the theories we use to analyse and criticize the world, even films like *The Matrix*, are themselves still socially conditioned. All our fantasies, all our most intimate thoughts and nightmares, are given to us by society. There is no such place as 'outside society'.

Durkheim documents this principle in a number of ways. His most famous example is the case of suicide. (You will remember that we discussed this case in Chapter 1, when we spoke of the sociological imagination.) Durkheim's concern in his work on suicide is to consider an act which, on the face of it, appears to be a most private and intimate one. This is the case of an individual whose life has become completely unbearable due to some set of accidental circumstances and who decides to take his own life. (Let us assume for a moment that he is a man.) Quite frequently these circumstances have to do with financial problems or matters of the heart. People often commit suicide because they are experiencing financial difficulties or problems in their sexual relationships.

Durkheim proceeds to show how this apparently very personal act is in fact deeply influenced by broad social conditions, whether that man is married or not, whether he is Jewish

The son of a Jewish Rabbi, **Emile Durkheim** was born in 1858 in Alsace, France. He died in 1916 during the First World War. His major works include *The Division of Labour* (1893), *The Rules of Sociological Method* (1895), *Suicide* (1897), and *The Elementary Forms of Religious Life* (1912).

or Catholic or Protestant, whether he lives in an urban or rural environment. These (macro-) factors, says Durkheim, are much more influential in pushing him to commit suicide than the particular problem facing him. His decision is deeply connected to social conditions, more particularly, the presence or absence of support structures, which might be religious, family or community structures. These factors shape people's decisions without their knowing about it.

This drive to show the major influence of society on individual action is a continuing theme throughout Durkheim's life, and indeed, in all macro-theory.

The second factor, *constraint*, by contrast, refers to the moral influence which society exercises over me. As a son in a family I am pushed, socialized, threatened, urged, persuaded that I have certain rights and certain duties. I have to act like a son. I may resist these obligations to some degree, but even resisting them assumes that they have a force over me. I cannot escape that influence completely.

In short, says Durkheim, society exists out there. It exists independently of me and exerts considerable influence over me; it makes me what I am.

There is very little of me that can escape that influence, which exists outside of or prior to society. I have very little pre-social biological or genetic conditioning that can stand up against society. Even my 'standing up' against society is itself conditioned by society.

Durkheim's third principle, *emergence*, is the process by which social elements combine to produce something new, something that did not exist before. In explaining this, Durkheim uses the example of hydrogen and oxygen, two gases, which, when they combine chemically, produce something quite different, water, which is a liquid. Likewise, when a number of individual people are combined in a particular way they produce a soccer team, or a family, or a whole society, and this influences their behaviour in quite significant ways.

For Durkheim, therefore, from social combination emerges something more than the separate individuals who constitute it, something which has a profound influence on the individuals who make it up.

Positive functions

Functionalist theory has that name because it places consider-able emphasis on the positive benefits that flow from aspects of society, that is, their functions. The easiest way to understand this is by looking at the human body. It is made up of a range of very different parts: hands, feet, head, stomach, legs, and so on. Each of these fits into a bigger and fairly harmonious whole. Each plays a different part in keeping that whole func-tioning. Stomachs digest food and provide the fuel from which the body derives energy; legs provide mobility.

So it is also in society. Each part of society, according to functionalists, contributes to the ongoing existence of the whole. Families, for example, reproduce the members of society by physically producing children, and by teaching them the basic values of society. Religion confirms and strengthens those basic values, and provides answers to troubling existential questions about birth and death, origin and meaning. Without these contributions society would not be able to exist.

For functionalists, emphasis on functions also answers ques-tions about system integration and order. How are the various parts of society co-ordinated? How do they stay in balance and harmony? Why do they not clash and conflict and undermine each other? The answer has partly to do with a common basic belief system, which we mentioned above, as well as with the positive benefits that each part of the system brings to it.

Criticisms of functionalism

As we might expect by now, functionalism has been subjected to considerable critique. First of all, let us look at the basic difference between functionalism and Marxism. For Marxists, society is a fundamentally conflictual entity. It is held together by the power which the ruling class exercises over it. It is an important criticism of functionalism that it downplays, even ignores, conflict in society. So, for example, functionalists wish to say that society is held together by a common value system. But we all know that many perfectly viable societies include groups with disparate religions, different cultures or

Question

In many ways Durkheim's theory on externality, constraint and emergence is very similar to Marx's views on the relationship between the individual and society. But there are also important differences. Can you name the differences?

41

clashing interests. For Durkheim, conflict was a form of social illness, something that was temporarily wrong and which could be healed.

Diagram adapted from D. Kendall, Sociology in Our Times *(1st edition), 1996, Wadsworth, ISBN 0534210244.*

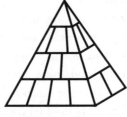

Functionalism

Marxism

Some writers also criticize functionalists for putting together an impossible causal sequence. What they mean by that is that the existence of a social institution is explained by its contribution to society. So, for example, as we have seen above, religion is seen to exist in society because it strengthens the basic value system. The problem is that the positive benefit that flows from the institution is seen to cause it to come into being. Or, to put it differently, what happens *after* an institution comes into existence explains the *earlier event* of its origin or why it continues to exist. However, something that comes later cannot cause something that comes earlier.

Durkheim was quite aware of this problem and he was careful to distinguish between functionalist argument and causal argument. Functionalist argument, for Durkheim, explains an institution's results. Causal argument explains where it comes from. And these two forms of argument should not be confused.

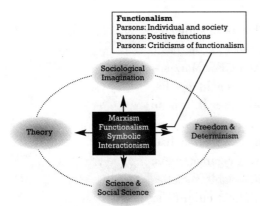

Talcott Parsons

Being a functionalist, Parsons was profoundly influenced by the work of Emile Durkheim. Many of the themes broached by Durkheim are taken forward and elaborated by Parsons. So we shall see that Parsons, like Durkheim, also addresses the issues of the relationship between individual and society, the problems of social change and social solidarity, and the functional relationship between parts of a system.

Parsons's work has been developed and refined by some of his students like Robert Merton and Neil Smelser, and by later neofunctionalists like Jeffrey Alexander and Niklas Luhmann.

Positive functions

We have seen that for Durkheim, social systems are sustained (although not created) by the positive functions which parts play for wholes. Specific parts of society can then be analysed in terms of their contributions to the whole. Parsons follows this principle but takes it a step further.

Systems, says Parsons, have certain basic needs without which they would not be able to exist. Thus, for example, there must be new members of society to replace those who die – there has to be reproduction. Those new members of society also have to learn how things are done in that society and why; in other words, there has to be socialization into the customs and values of that society.

This generates Parsons's famous AGIL schema. In order to survive, societies need:

- to *adapt* to their environment;
- to pursue and achieve the *goals* which society sets for itself;
- to *integrate* and co-ordinate the various system units; and
- to sustain the cultural patterns of society and to resolve the conflicts in it; this he called *latency*.

Each of these functions also corresponds to subsystems in society. Thus, adaptation indicates the *economic* subsystem which secures resources for society from the environment and distributes them in society. Goal attainment refers to the *political* subsystem through which goals for society are decided and resources allocated for their achievement. Integration entails mainly the *legal* subsystem in balancing the various subsystem needs. Latency, finally, points to the various *socialization* processes (like families and schools) whereby a society's culture is transmitted to its members.

Talcott Parsons, arguably the greatest American sociologist, was born in 1902 in Colorado, and died in 1979. He started working at Harvard in 1927 as a junior instructor and remained there until his death 50 years later. His major works included *The Structure of Social Action* (1937), *The Social System* (1951), and *Economy and Society* (with Neil J. Smelser) (1956). A number of quite famous sociologists studied under Parsons, taking his principles forward in important ways. They were Robert Merton, Kingsley Davis, Wilbert Moore, Marion Levy and Neil Smelser.

Criticisms of functionalism

If you look at Parsons's argument more carefully, you will see that there are serious problems. Parsons argues that, like other biological organisms, certain functions are needed for society to survive. Since any society under examination is obviously there and has survived, all of these basic needs must have been satisfied. But, and here is the problem, what would a society look like that had not survived, because societies do not literally 'die'?

Thus, societies change shape, go through revolutions, reform and continue. What would a society look like where any one of these functions had broken down; where, for example, the legal system had collapsed? Or the political system had been taken over by the military? Those societies would clearly continue to exist, albeit in a less coherent and harmonious way. The communist states in Eastern Europe shifted quite dramatically after 1989, but they did not disappear or 'die'.

In the end, Parsons's list of essential basic needs is a highly abstract, somewhat arbitrary list, which is impossible to check in reality.

Functionalism, in summary, is a theory about how society and its various parts hang together in a state of balance. It tries to show why the social system does not descend into complete chaos, why various groups in society do not exist in perpetual conflict. Society, according to functionalism, is like a body in which a whole range of very different parts all contribute to the bigger whole, all driven by a similar value system, all dependent on one another.

4 | Symbolic Interactionism

In Chapter 2 we noted that Marxism is a curious theory because it is still so intimately tied to its founder, Karl Marx, even bearing his name. Just how curious this is can most clearly be seen in the case of symbolic interactionist theory. This theory is directly linked to the work of George Herbert Mead.

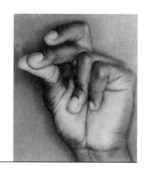

But unlike Marx he is only one among a series of symbolic interactionist thinkers, which includes writers like Erving Goffmann and Herbert Blumer. Symbolic interactionism is itself also only one in a range of microsociologies which includes ethnomethodology, phenomenology and hermeneutics. These theories and their principal authors are listed in the table below.

THEORY	MAIN WRITER
Symbolic interactionism	George Herbert Mead
Hermeneutics	Hans-Georg Gadamer
Phenomenology	Alfred Schutz
Ethnomethodology	Harold Garfinkel

These theories all have a common foundation in their emphasis on meaning, on individual actors, on individual identity and consciousness, and on small-scale face-to-face situations, rather than on larger-scale structures. In this section I will concentrate on symbolic interactionism.

I shall start with a discussion of Max Weber's two principles of social analysis in microsociology. The first emphasizes individual meaning as the basis of analysis. The second emphasizes the individual actor as opposed to social structure. Here we see that social structure is derived from individual meaning and from individuals in interaction. Both of these principles are in opposition to those of Durkheim and Marx.

From here we move to George Herbert Mead, the real father of symbolic interactionism. From Mead we take also two principles. The first focuses on action and behaviour in constructing meaning. This is the principle of pragmatism. The second principle sees the self as the product of interaction with significant others in society. We experience ourselves through the responses of other people. For Mead, the self is split between two elements in conversation with each other, a spontaneous 'I' and a controlling, socially conscious 'me'.

In the last section I consider the intriguing impact of these theories on South African sociological thinking about the identities of migrant mineworkers.

Max Weber

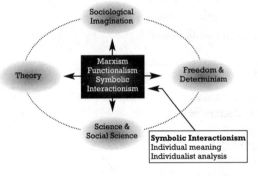

Historically, an important root of microsociological theory, in general, and symbolic interactionism, in particular, lies in the work of Max Weber. Throughout his work Max Weber insisted on two basic and linked principles, namely that sociological analysis must start with an interpretation of the meaning which individuals attach to their actions (what Weber termed *verstehen*), and that sociological analysis is first and foremost the analysis of individuals.

Individual meaning

Let us start with the principle of *verstehen*, or understanding. This entails the necessity, for Weber, of interpretation. Thus, if I see a man chopping wood, I cannot assume that I know what he is up to. He might be simply gathering fuel for a fire, or he might be cutting building materials to the right size, or he might be exercising his upper body, or he might be letting off steam as a result of a quarrel with his wife. Just as in the case of the sharp jab we looked at before, a simple action can carry a range of different meanings. Each of these meanings would have very different implications for his interaction with other people.

But how do we come to understand other people? What gives us the ability to interpret their meaning? Weber was concerned that interpretation should not be based on any indefinable and vague process of intuition. Human action could be defined according to a range of clear categories based on their motives. Thus, Weber distinguished four classes of social action and each of these action types had a clearly discernible and understandable logic:

- *traditional action*, which was determined by individuals' habitual and customary ways of doing things. Our man chopping wood would in this case be doing it because this is what his father and grandfather had always done;
- *affectual action*, which served to express emotion. This is the case where our woodchopper is giving vent to his frustration;
- *means-end rationality*, which indicates the harnessing of particular resources and situations to particular goals. Here chopping wood would be part of a calculated plan to build a house;
- *value-rationality*, which entails acting out a belief in a value for its own sake regardless of cost. In this instance chopping wood might be a religious act symbolizing a sacred event without any material gain attached to it.

Although each of these categories could be applied to particular actions, said Weber, it was also possible that actions were a combination of all of these types.

Individualist analysis

The second and linked principle that Weber emphasized was that social analysis is first and foremost the analysis of individuals.

It is only by an analysis of individuals and their meaningful actions that a bigger cumulative picture of society can be built up. So, for example, said Weber, individuals in interaction with each other over a longer period of time could come to see their interaction as a matter of fixed routine. And if this routine carried over from one generation to another, it could become imbued with 'the force of history'. It would then be seen as traditional action, the class of action we considered earlier, carried forward by the approval of ancestors and revered forefathers. In this way you can see how Weber gradually built up individual action and interaction into regular social structure. Structure for Weber is the result and the sedimentation of the activities of particular agents.

Durkheim against Weber

You will remember that this is diametrically opposed to Durkheim's approach. For Durkheim, individual action is determined by broader social structures, and social analysis begins with structure, not with individual meaning. In fact, Durkheim had very little use for individual meaning. How do we then come to terms with these contradictory views from two of sociology's greatest thinkers? Each of them seems to have extremely plausible arguments. Here is one way out of the dilemma.

In their writing you will see that neither of these thinkers consistently followed their own principles. In the case of suicide, for example, Durkheim smuggled meaning back into his analysis by showing that it was the presence or absence of support in individuals' lives which determined whether they committed suicide or not. Put differently, when individuals experienced the meaning of structures around them as supportive, nurturing or understanding, the impetus towards self-destruction was much weakened. In Weber's case, by contrast, most of his work in the end was not about individuals and their personal mental states, as one might have expected, but about broader social phenomena like culture, capitalism and class. He wrote (quite pessimistically) about bureaucratic structures as an 'iron cage' from which there was no escape.

This does not mean that we can throw both of their arguments out of the window. Rather the opposite: it means that both are in fact valid. For their treatment of empirical and historical material shows just how difficult it is to stick to one of these principles to the exclusion of the other.

In other words, we can accept the principle that social analysis must take account of meaning, and also the principle that structures are extremely influential in people's lives in ways that they are unaware of. The two can be easily combined by saying that structures are not always external to individuals. Through the process of socialization they become internalized, which means that individual actors experience social structures as meaningful. The way in which researchers gain evidence of structures is through the way people meaningfully experience them. Structural perspectives and meaning perspectives are therefore deeply intertwined.

How does this compare to the solutions to the dilemmas of theoretical pluralism which we discussed in Chapter 1? Is this eclecticism?

George Herbert Mead

The work of George Herbert Mead took Weber's principles forward and adjusted them in important ways. Like other micro-sociologists, Mead focused on meaning, on the individual, on aspects of the individual like the self, and on the interaction between individuals. But, as we shall see, Mead was noted among microsociologists for two reasons: first, he emphasized the dominant influence of society over the actions of the individual, and, secondly, he emphasized action and behaviour.

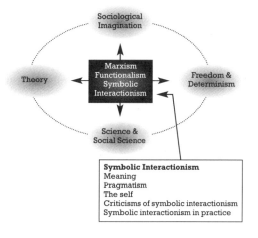

Meaning

Meaning is fundamental to all microsociological writing. As we have seen in Chapter 1, human beings do not respond 'automatically' to stimuli. Even the most physical of stimuli, like a sharp prick, is interpreted as a scorpion sting, or a thorn, or a jab from a syringe. It has a particular meaning. More importantly, and unlike the picture that macrosociology paints of us, human beings do not 'automatically' play the roles which society allocates to them. They do not respond to structural constraints 'unthinkingly'. All such participation is continually interpreted, constructed in a meaningful way, negotiated, put together as part of an ongoing process.

So, for example, there may be social expectations and rules for how one acts as a daughter. But each individual interprets this in a different way, makes something particular of it, bends the rules just a little, and sometimes more than a little.

Pragmatism

An important thing to understand about Mead is that he was a *pragmatist*. In philosophy, which is where the term comes from, this means something quite different from its everyday meaning. If you called someone a pragmatist, you would probably mean that this person had few fixed moral principles. As Mead used it, however, pragmatism emphasizes the centrality of action in understanding individual members of society. Contrary to certain strands of phenomenology, there is, for Mead, no such thing as pure consciousness. Consciousness is a process whereby individuals actively engage with their environments, adapting their responses to it. Human consciousness only exists in interaction with the world. One is only conscious of something, and with a view to acting in relationship to it.

Imagine yourself waking up in the morning. When you first 'become conscious', you are not just conscious. You are immediately conscious of your body, the fact that you are breathing, that your feet are warm or cold, that your side feels stiff from lying on it for too long. One of your first thoughts on waking will be what the time is: whether it is time to get up and go to work, or, if it is the weekend, that you can relax a while longer. In short, your consciousness is *of something*, and of some *behaviour* that goes with it.

For example, think about a chair. There is a staggering variety of objects that we call chairs. They differ in shape, size, texture, structure and material. What binds them all is our abstract idea of a chair, but particularly the fact that chairs involve sitting. It is the action implied that makes a key difference.

The self

Another important facet in Mead's sociology is his notion of the *self*. Theories of the self are central to all microsociological theories. For Mead, as one would expect from a pragmatist, the self develops in human beings in response to, and in adaptation to, the social world. People acquire a sense of self in interaction with other people. The self is an ongoing process. It is not a static entity. You learn who you are by observing other people's responses to you. Your experience of yourself is therefore an indirect one. Mead's American colleague, Charles H. Cooley, coined the term 'the looking glass self' for this aspect, since you see yourself reflected in the responses of people around you. Your experience of yourself is therefore an indirect one. It is translated to you through the social environment.

That means that you also experience yourself just as you experience other people, as an object. This is also the same way in which you experience your body. You are a body, but you also have a body. You use your body just as you would use a tool. That is why tools can be experienced as extensions of your body. The way you experience yourself using a hammer is no different in principle from the way you experience yourself using your own hand.

This sense of yourself as an object is expressed in language by the word 'me'. I can experience me/myself as an object. The fact that this experience goes through other people's responses indicates that my sense of 'me' comes from society. It is the way you adapt and accommodate yourself to society.

'Me' is different from 'I'. For Mead, 'I' is the way you experience yourself immediately and spontaneously. The 'I' is the source of creativity and innovation in people's interaction with society. In action, and in interaction with other people, these two parts of yourself are in continual dialogue. They speak to each other.

Let us take an example. Through the 'I' you experience impulses to action. You feel hungry, or attracted to someone, or tired. Each of these impulses entails some kind of action. If I

Question

Earlier we spoke about society's shaping of the individual through socialization and internalization processes. How do you think Cooley's 'looking glass self' differs from those notions?

feel hungry, I want to pick up this apple from this bowl and eat it. If I feel attracted to someone, I want to go over and engage that person in conversation. If I feel tired, I want to close my eyes, lie back and go to sleep. But each of these actions occurs in a social situation. The apple does not belong to me. Nor does the attractive person, who may be married to someone else. When I feel tired I may be in a meeting.

In these situations the 'me' side of myself weighs up possible alternative actions, considers what they would look like to other people and finally decides on a particular option. Here we have all the elements of Mead's self: an 'I' and a 'me' in conversation with each other, self as an ongoing process of orienting your action to the immediate environment, and the influence of society in tension with the will and choices of the individual. For Mead, then, the self both shapes and is shaped by society.

Criticisms of symbolic interactionism

But there is something missing here: Mead says very little about the broad macro-structures of society and how they arise. How, for example, in our example of the grass plain, a path would accumulate sedimented and layered meanings by which it would bind people to use it in particular ways. It is true, as we saw above, that Mead acknowledges the prime influence of society in shaping identity. But how does this society arise in the interaction of meanings and individuals. It is an ongoing critique of Mead that he spent very little effort in trying to explain this aspect of society. Maybe he thought that these aspects had been addressed by other theorists. Whatever he thought, this is often seen as a gap in Mead's theory which other symbolic interactionists have needed to fill.

Symbolic interactionism in practice

How does this quite abstract set of principles play out in practice? In the South African context it has given rise to an intriguing debate around the influence of labour compounds on the identities and selves of mineworkers. South African mines have a history of housing in labour compounds, to which single men had travelled from rural areas or other countries to take up work. By any standard these institutions operated under extremely strict controls. Above ground there were detailed rules for behaviour concerning issues like fighting, sex, drugs, eating, cooking, laundry, and so on. These were enforced by an elaborate set of controls. Under ground, where the physical danger from blasting and from rock falls is extreme, the discipline was even tighter. Workers operated in teams with team-leaders and 'boss-boys'. Many writers have depicted labour compounds as 'total institutions', that is, institutions like prisons or mental asylums which exercise strong and detailed authority over all aspects of inmates' lives.

The question that arises in these situations is this: To what degree can rural mineworkers maintain a sense of personal autonomy and identity? They are people who often come from tribal and traditional backgrounds in the Lesotho highlands, Botswana or the (then) Transkei. How do rural identities fare under extreme pressure from a total institution?

There has been considerable debate among writers on this issue. Some writers, particularly those influenced by Erving Goffman, feel that miners became 'men of two worlds' with two quite distinct identities, one rural and one mine. In this case they were seen as having very little defense against institutional pressure. When they were in the rural areas, they thought and behaved like traditional rural men. But in the mine compound they assumed different clothing (both literally and figuratively), and they had quite different attitudes to sexuality, authority, obedience and ethnic culture.

Other writers, who have been influenced by Alfred Schutz's phenomenology, have felt that rural workers mobilized a range of rural cultural items, like myths and legends, to maintain an independent and strongly rural sense of self. They 'worked the system' in agile and creative ways, exhibiting resistance to the invasiveness of mine culture and behaviour. In this view they were able to maintain their original sense of self, and return unscathed to their village homes.

A third group of writers take what would be Mead's own position between these two extremes. In this scenario migrants both shaped, and were shaped by, mine institutions and values. So, for example, institutions of authority on the mine showed strong tribal influences, as did the ethnic differences and conflicts between workers. Thus, internal heads of mine compounds were called *indunas*. In this way miners' tribal influence made itself felt. On the other hand, they also moulded themselves quite sharply to the demands of mine work. They were subjected to and adapted to hard and harrowing working conditions which demanded strenuous physical exertion and continual watchfulness for rockfalls.

In the diagram below, then, Goffman's migrants oscillate between a (round) rural area, and a (triangular) mine compound. Shutz's migrants, by contrast, stay consistently (round) rural in both situations. Mead's migrants, finally, start rural but end as a mixture of rural and mine influences.

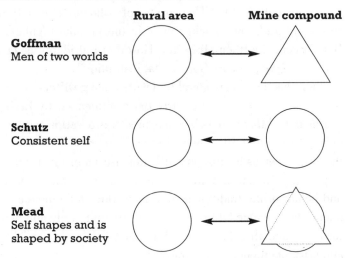

In summary, then, symbolic interactionism, in contrast to both Marxism and functionalism, is a micro-theory. It focuses on the smaller, more immediate world of individuals, their interactions, their identities. It emphasizes that society is built on the accumulated actions and interactions of individual actors. It shows how these individuals construct a sense of self in society and through society. It underlines not only the centrality of meaning but also the slipperiness of meaning. It allows for a far greater degree of choice and freedom in the connection between individual and society.

5 | A Comparative Conclusion

In this final chapter I want to put the three theories we have been considering alongside each other: Marxism, functionalism, symbolic interactionism. What are the critical differences between them? Is there a neat way we can summarize their similarities and contrasts? There are two ways we can attempt this comparison.

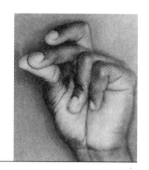

One is to take a practical example and show how each theory in turn would go about explaining things. The other is to construct a three-column table with the aspects of each theory neatly placed alongside each other.

Let us start with a particular practical example. You will remember that earlier we used the example of a group of people living on the edge of a very wide grassy plain, and how they gradually came to find a path across it, and to establish that path as a central part of their living.

What would happen if a Marxist were considering this example? Remember the fundamental elements of Marxist theory: the economic/production base of society, class conflict, exploitation.

Question

Take a moment now to think how you would do this exercise using Marxist concepts.

Here is my own attempt. A *Marxist* would start by considering the system of production in that particular society. Suppose it was a pastoral society in which people had already learnt the skill of domesticating animals and certain plants. In other words, they were elementary agriculturalists, but not so elementary that there was no surplus production. That would mean that some individuals could specialize in particular skills and crafts, some could live off the labour of others. There would then be chiefs and headmen. As a ruling class in this society they would own more cattle and have more land than 'ordinary' members of society. One of these headmen, or perhaps the chief himself, would control access to the important path across the grass plain. He would make people pay to use the path. This privilege would ensure a continuing source of income for the chief. The path would link the group on the edge of the grass plain to another group over the hill, and it would help to set up trading links between the two places. Since the chief was the wealthiest man in the village, most of the goods being traded would also belong to him, and he would become wealthier and wealthier – so wealthy, in fact, that he might consider taking over the other village for his own purposes.

What would a *functionalist* do with this story? Remember that functionalists, by contrast, would start with a society's value system, show how its various institutions, roles and norms interwove with each other, and how various parts of society stayed in equilibrium and benefited the whole. A functionalist would then begin by asking about the society's system of beliefs and religion. How does religion explain the origins of the group, in fact, the origins of human kind? How do human beings, in this belief, fit into the cosmos? Let us suppose then that this group believes that their chiefs are descended from a divine spirit, and that each year the chief is required by age-old tradition to lead his people in a sacred ritual to bring rain and to make the grass grow on the plain for their cattle. In this ritual he walks down the path when the moon is full, and sacrifices a goat. (The word 'sacrifice' originally meant 'to make sacred'.) This ritual has a profound effect on people because it binds them as a group into a common system of beliefs: it accentuates their particular identity and confirms their common historical roots, and it gives their lives meaning by showing them how they connect to the spirits and the forefathers.

Let us think now how a *symbolic interactionist* would look at this society. For this exercise we would need to descend from the broad societal perspective, and consider particular individuals: how they construct meaning in their lives, and how they negotiate the influence and power of other members of society. Imagine, then, a woman, married to a commoner in the village, in other words her husband is not a chief or headman. She knows that her husband is required to pay tribute to the

Question

How is that for a start? Do you think you can continue the story? Think, for example, how conflict between the chief and his people might worsen. And what would happen then?

Question

Can you take this further? What role would families, as opposed to religion, play? How would one think about economics?

chief each time he uses the path. She knows that traditional custom does not easily permit her, as a woman, to question her husband's authority, and even less that of the chief. Nevertheless, she is clever. She gets her husband to do things by telling him that his favourite baby son requires it, by showing him how other men have gained advantage over him, by telling him gently critical stories about some of his acquaintances. (These are strategies which she actually learnt from her mother and has now elaborated upon.) So, while she is not a feminist in anything like the modern sense of the word, she has begun to be creative with her own position and her own identity as a woman. She would never dream that women should become chiefs, for example, or that things should be turned around so that women dominate men. Nothing quite so revolutionary, because, after all, she is a product of her society. But she can make a difference.

Question

What would happen, from an interactionist perspective, do you think, if she began to talk to and influence other women? Could this result in a structural change, or not?

Now, let us try another type of comparing. The table on the following page is a quick comparison of the three theories that we have been discussing, and also a brief summary of that discussion. It compares Marxism, functionalism and symbolic interactionism in their views on a range of basic sociological issues (listed down the left-hand column). So, for example, the relationship between individual and society has been a prominent theme from the beginning of this book. In Chapter 1, I defined both structure and agency and showed how we might think of them as interacting through the notion of *mutual constitution*. Marx saw them in a spiral of dialectical interaction, but nevertheless thought that individuals were powerfully determined by structure. Functionalism, similarly, sees the individual as substantially determined by structure. Symbolic interactionism, for its part, sees individuals as both shaping and being shaped by society.

THEMES	MARXISM	FUNCTIONALISM	SYMBOLIC INTERACTIONISM
Level of analysis	**Macrolevel**	**Macrolevel**	**Microlevel**
Individual and society	Dialectic spiral between individual & society; but society determines the individual	Society external to individual, society determines the individual	Individual shapes and is shaped by society; structures grow by continued habitual interaction
Basis of system-relating	Base and superstructure	Positive functions; interdependence	Subjective perceptions of order
Determinant factor	Economics	Cultural values	Individual meaning
Criticisms	Economic determinism	Ignores conflict; problems in functionalist argument	Ignores structural constraint

And, finally, on the opposite page you will see a diagram that pulls together all the topics that we have discussed in this book. We started in Chapter 1 with the very basic diagram. At regular intervals along the way we have used icons to illustrate how each particular topic fits into the bigger picture. Now you can see the whole journey we have covered at a glance: how the three theories, Marxism, functionalism and symbolic interactionism, have addressed the big questions of sociology, namely the sociological imagination, the individual and society, social science and science, and theory. Clearly, we have spent more time on some questions than others, but, within the space of this small book, that is all that has been possible.

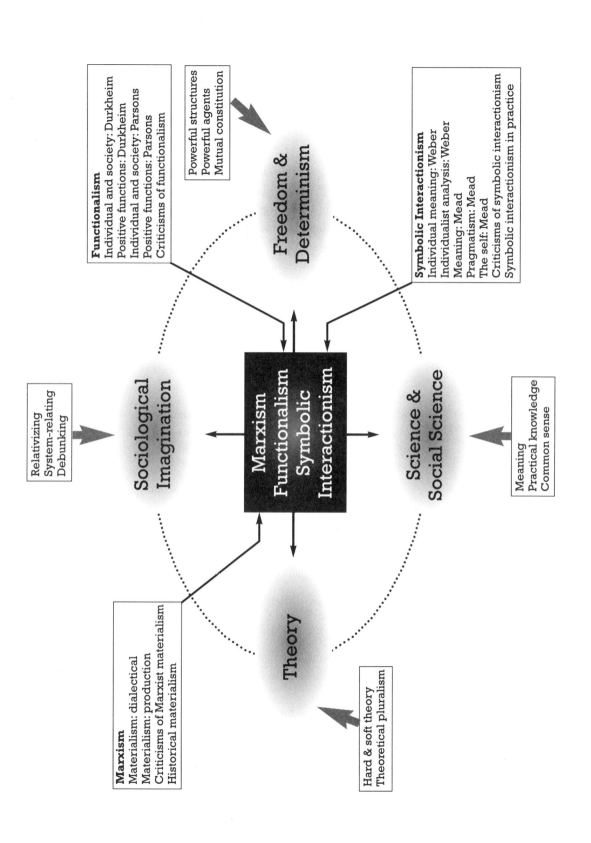

Functionalism
Individual and society: Durkheim
Positive functions: Durkheim
Individual and society: Parsons
Positive functions: Parsons
Criticisms of functionalism

Powerful structures
Powerful agents
Mutual constitution

Symbolic Interactionism
Individual meaning: Weber
Individualist analysis: Weber
Meaning: Mead
Pragmatism: Mead
The self: Mead
Criticisms of symbolic interactionism
Symbolic interactionism in practice

Freedom &
Determinism

Relativizing
System-relating
Debunking

Sociological
Imagination

Marxism
Functionalism
Symbolic
Interactionism

Science &
Social Science

Meaning
Practical knowledge
Common sense

Marxism
Materialism: dialectical
Materialism: production
Criticisms of Marxist materialism
Historical materialism

Theory

Hard & soft theory
Theoretical pluralism

Exercises

In Chapter 1 we introduced certain big themes in sociology, which we have continued to pursue throughout the book. I have chosen the first, and arguably the biggest of these themes – the relationship between individual and society – and constructed some exercises around it. Of course, we could ask a whole lot more questions around the other big themes but we do not have space for all of those here. If you wish to explore the other big themes in more detail, visit the Oxford University Press website: *www.oup.com/za/sociology*.

More about questions

Exercises come in different forms, some are easier and some are more difficult. The easier ones (Level A questions) typically ask you to do things like:
- 'define' concepts
- 'explain what' X says about something, or
- 'summarize' what Y says about something else.

This is relatively easy because it asks you simply to understand what a writer is saying and to express it in your own words.

Slightly more difficult questions (Level B questions) will ask you to:
- 'explain how' A links with B according to Marx or Durkheim
- 'compare and contrast' Weber and Parsons, or
- 'apply' Mead's ideas in a particular situation.

These questions take some extra thought because you are being asked to transpose ideas from one situation to another. You may also be asked to:
- 'construct a careful argument about ...'

In this case you are required to put together a coherent story which has logical and reasoned steps which follow from one another.

The most difficult, and the most interesting, questions (Level C) will ask you:

- to 'construct your own examples' of a particular concept
- to 'discuss/critically evaluate' the ideas or arguments of, say, Durkheim or Weber, or
- 'whether or not you agree with' this or that view.

These are more difficult because you have to start being creative and mobilize your own independent thoughts. In the assessment of academic work, this skill is also considered to be the most valuable.

Theme: Individual and society

Level A

1 Give brief definitions of the following terms, and where appropriate indicate which writer uses them:

agent
structure
mutual constitution of agent and structure
materialism: the spiral of change
externality
constraint
emergence
collective conscience
verstehen
pragmatism
the looking glass self
the difference between the 'I' and the 'me'.

Level B

Explain how:
1 individual and society interact in Marx's materialist spiral of change;
2 new things emerge when, according to Durkheim, social elements are arranged in a particular way;
3 according to Mead, individuals construct an identity by interaction with significant others in society.

Compare and contrast:
4 the interaction of individual and society as seen by Marx and Durkheim;
5 the place of meaning for sociological analysis in Durkheim and Weber.

Explain how:
6 Durkheim debunks the idea that suicide is about matters of finance and of the heart;
7 Marx debunks the notion of the profit-motive as an inherent part of human nature.

Level C

Do you agree with:
1 Marx's view that society is based on conflict, explain why;
2 the functionalist view that ultimately societies are held together by agreement on basic values, give reasons;
3 the functionalist view that societies can be seen as a body, explain why.

Longer essay question

1 Some writers argue that structure determines agency (or that society determines the individual). Others argue the opposite. Some writers wish to balance the two in equal measure. Which of these arguments do you support, and why? In your answer, give examples of each of these arguments, show where you think they fall short, and give reasons for the views that you have chosen.

Glossary

affectual action action which serves to express emotion (Weber)

agent an individual or group actor in society

base the economic foundation on which other parts of society are built, consisting of the class structures and the forces of production (Marx)

collective consciousness the consensus among people on the basic values of society (Durkheim)

constraint the moral influence which society exercises over individuals (Durkheim)

debunking the activity which reveals the private, grubby, questionable side of social life behind the public image

decentred self the view of an individual as a collection of quite disparate bits, substantially influenced by unconscious and hidden urges and also by the structures of society

dialectical materialism when two elements of society, for example, the individual and society, are in interaction, mutually influencing each other, and by this process setting up a spiral of continual change (Marx)

eclecticism a view which says there is no correct and exhaustive theory; sociologists should have at their disposal a range of theories to draw from, a different one for each different situation

emergence the process by which social elements combine to produce something new, something that did not exist before (Durkheim)

externality the principle that society exists prior to our entry into it, and will continue to exist after our departure from it (Durkheim)

historical materialism Marx's theory of historical change, based on the movement from one form of society to another

materialism the principle that production is the foundation of society; see also dialectical materialism (Marx)

means-end rationality the harnessing of particular resources and situations to particular goals (Weber)

methodological individualism the theory that all aspects of society must be explained first by reference to individual members of society

mutual constitution of agent and structure the situation in which agents and structures depend on each other for their existence

practical knowledge skills which cannot be expressed in words

pragmatism the centrality of action in understanding individual members of society (Mead)

relativizing the process of putting social phenomena into broader historical and cultural perspective

socialization the process by which individuals internalize and learn the values, culture and practices of their society

society a group of people with some internal coherence and a discernible boundary between themselves and other groups

structure a regular pattern of behaviour in society; the grooves of accustomed, habituated activity into which people's lives fit

superstructure those aspects of society like religion, ideology, and politics which are significantly determined by the base (Marx)

surplus the resources available when production of basic resources goes beyond immediate needs (Marx)

system-relating the process of connecting social phenomena to their wider and broader contexts

the looking glass self the way in which you are reliant on seeing yourself reflected in the responses of people around you (Cooley)

theoretical pluralism the situation in which you have more than one theory that can be used to explain a phenomenon

traditional action individuals' habitual and customary ways of doing things (Weber)

value rationality acting out a belief in a value for its own sake regardless of cost (Weber)

verstehen the process of interpretation in sociological analysis (Weber)

Annotated Bibliography

Bauman, Z. (1990) *Thinking Sociologically*. Oxford: Basil Blackwell.

This is an intriguing and most unusual introduction to sociology. It is not written as a standard textbook but rather as something that the lay person would find interesting and accessible.

Berger, P. (1966) *Invitation to Sociology – A Humanistic Perspective*. Harmondsworth: Penguin Books.

Written a long time ago, this is still one of the classics of introductory sociology. It brims with enthusiasm and energy, and is full of intriguing insights. For those who want to pursue Berger's ideas in more sophisticated format, try *The Social Construction of Reality* by P. Berger and T. Luckmann.

Bruce, S. (1999) *Sociology: A Very Short Introduction*. Oxford: Oxford University Press.

A wonderfully written little book (very little – it fits in the palm of your hand) on the basic principles of sociology. It provides a few hours of enjoyable reading.

Craib, I. (1997) *Classical Social Theory: An Introduction to the Thoughts of Marx, Weber, Durkheim and Simmel*. Oxford: Oxford University Press.

This is a beautifully constructed book covering a restricted range of key topics in the writings of Marx, Weber, Durkheim and Simmel. If you want a comparative text on how these classical authors treat the notions of individual and society, social structure, social system and so on, you will find it done here with clarity and flair.

Giddens, A. (2001) *Sociology* (Fourth Edition). Cambridge: Polity Press.

This is a lucid and simply written introduction to sociology put together by one of the foremost modern theorists. It covers a wide range of topics, many of which are not found in other textbooks.

Haralambos & Holborn (2000) *Sociology: Themes and Perspectives* (Sixth Edition). London: Collins Educational.
This is probably the most thorough and detailed introductory sociology textbook on the market today. It has deservedly been through a number of editions and is now in its fifth.

Marshall, G. (1998) *A Dictionary of Sociology.* New York: Oxford University Press.
Having a sociological dictionary at your disposal is extremely useful in getting to know the discipline. This is one of the better ones.

Mills, Wright C. (1959) *The Sociological Imagination.* Harmondsworth: Penguin.
This is the book that started a whole industry of writing about the basic principles of sociology. It is an old classic but is still worth paging through.

Index

social science 2, 16–21
society
    see also structures
    definition 7
society and individual *see*
    individual and society
sociological imagination 1, 3–7
sociology
    nature of 1
    as social science 2, 16–21
structural determinist 34
structures 1, 7, 8–14, 15–16, 49,
    57, 58
suicide 8–9, 10–11, 39–40, 48
superstructure 32, 33, 34

surplus 35–36
symbolic interactionism 24, 45–46
    comparison to Marxism &
        functionalism 58, 59
    criticisms 52
    George Herbert Mead 49–52
    Max Weber 46–48
    practical example 56–57
    in South African context 52–54
system-relating 5–6

T
theological thinking 16, 20
theoretical pluralism 24–26
theory 2, 21–22

hard and soft 22–24
    theoretical pluralism 24–26
traditional action 47

V
value-rationality 47
value system 38, 41, 42, 43, 56
verstehen 46–47

W
Weber, Max 25–26
    comparison to Durkheim 48–49
    theory of symbolic interactionism
        45–48